Consider The Lilies Handbook | Your Guide to Lasting Serenity

Break Free from Anxiety and Discover Lasting Peace Through God's Unchanging Promises!

John A. Adams

Table of Contents

Chapter 1: Embracing Serenity

In our fast-paced world, filled with constant notifications and an ever-growing to-do list, finding serenity can often feel like an elusive dream. Yet, the quest for peace is not only possible but essential for our spiritual and emotional well-being. The key to unlocking this tranquility lies not in escaping our daily routines but in weaving moments of calm and reflection into the fabric of our lives. By turning to the timeless wisdom found in Scripture, we can discover a wellspring of comfort that refreshes our souls and renews our perspective. This chapter invites you to embark on a transformative journey toward serenity, a journey that does not require you to change your external circumstances but to deepen your internal connection to God's unchanging promises.

The Bible offers countless insights into the nature of peace, portraying it as a divine gift that surpasses all understanding. This peace is not contingent on the absence of trouble but on the presence of God. To embrace serenity in a chaotic world, we must first acknowledge our human tendency to seek control over our environment and circumstances. This inclination often leads to anxiety and unrest, as we struggle against the unpredictable currents of life. However, by recognizing that true peace comes from surrendering our fears and anxieties to God, we can begin to experience the stability and calm that comes from trusting in His sovereign care.

One practical step toward cultivating this trust is through reflective scripture journaling. This exercise involves selecting passages that speak to God's faithfulness and meditating on them, allowing their truths to sink deeply into our hearts. As we reflect on God's word, we are reminded of His steadfast presence in our lives, even amidst turmoil. This practice not only strengthens our faith but also shifts our focus from our problems to God's promises.

Another powerful tool in our pursuit of serenity is guided scripture meditation. This involves spending quiet time in prayerful reflection on specific biblical texts, asking the Holy Spirit to illuminate their meaning and application in our lives. Through this contemplative process, we can gain insights and encouragement that help us navigate the challenges we face with a sense of peace and assurance.

Scripture-based affirmations serve as daily reminders of God's love, power, and provision. By affirming these truths, we reinforce our identity as beloved children of God, which in turn, fosters a deep sense of security and peace. These affirmations can be personalized and repeated throughout the day, especially in moments of stress or uncertainty, to remind us of the unshakeable peace that is ours in Christ.

As we integrate these practices into our daily routines, we begin to notice a shift in our internal landscape. The chaos of the world around us no longer has the same power to disturb our peace, for we have learned to anchor our hearts in the truth of God's word. This chapter lays the foundation for a life characterized by serenity, a life where peace flows not from the absence of problems but from the presence of God amidst them.

The journey towards serenity also involves the cultivation of a prayer life that acknowledges God's sovereignty in every aspect of our existence. Prayer, a direct line to the Divine, allows us to lay down our burdens and find rest in the assurance of His omnipotence and omniscience. It's in the quiet moments of prayer that we often find the strength to endure our trials, not because our circumstances have necessarily changed, but because our perspective has shifted. We recognize that we are not alone in our struggles; we are supported and sustained by a power far greater than our own.

To deepen this connection, engaging in prayerful visualization techniques can be immensely beneficial. This practice involves envisioning our worries being lifted away by God's loving hands, replaced with His peace and comfort. Visualization not only aids in reducing anxiety but also strengthens our faith as we 'see' God's promises in action. This act of faith reinforces our belief in God's ability to intervene and transform our reality, providing a solid foundation for lasting serenity.

Moreover, incorporating scripture-based affirmations into our prayer life amplifies the impact of our prayers. Speaking God's promises out loud, declaring His goodness and faithfulness over our lives, acts as a powerful counter to the lies and fears that often plague our minds. These affirmations remind us of who God is and who we are in Him, realigning our thoughts with His truth.

Community also plays a pivotal role in our journey towards peace. Sharing our struggles and victories with fellow believers provides encouragement and accountability. As we open up about our journeys, we often find that we are not as isolated in our experiences as we might have thought. This sense of fellowship not only diminishes the weight of our burdens but also mirrors the communal nature of the early church, as depicted in the Acts of the Apostles. Engaging in group Bible study or prayer meetings can further enhance our understanding of God's peace, providing a collective experience of His presence that fortifies our individual walks.

Lastly, the practice of gratitude shifts our focus from what we lack to the abundance we already possess in Christ. Keeping a gratitude journal, where we record daily the blessings God has poured into our lives, cultivates a heart of thankfulness. This practice not only combats discontent and anxiety but also opens our eyes to the myriad ways God is working in and around us. Recognizing and celebrating God's goodness, even in small things, anchors us more firmly in His peace.

In embracing these practices, we find that serenity is not a distant dream but a present reality available to us in Christ. Through reflective scripture journaling, guided scripture meditation, prayerful visualization, and the cultivation of gratitude and community, we learn to navigate the chaos of the world with grace and peace. It is in the daily commitment to these practices that we discover the depth of God's peace, a peace that transcends all understanding and guards our hearts and minds in Christ Jesus.

Understanding Anxiety Through Faith

In the Scriptures, we find a profound understanding of human emotions, including those that unsettle us. Anxiety, a common experience among many, is not ignored in the biblical narrative. Instead, it is addressed with compassion and practical guidance. The Apostle Paul, in his letter to the Philippians, offers a directive that transcends time: "Do not be anxious about anything, but in every situation, by prayer and petition, with thanksgiving, present your requests to God." This instruction does not merely serve as a command to cease feeling anxious; it acknowledges the reality of our worries while steering us towards a solution grounded in faith and communication with the Divine.

Prayer emerges as a central theme in managing anxiety through a faith-based lens. It is not presented as a quick fix but as a relational process, a way of engaging with God about our deepest fears and concerns. Through prayer, we are invited to lay bare our vulnerabilities, knowing that we are heard and loved unconditionally. This act of faith does not negate the reality of our anxiety but positions it within the context of a relationship with a sovereign God who cares.

Scripture also plays a crucial role in addressing anxiety. The Psalms, for instance, are replete with expressions of distress, fear, and longing for peace. These ancient songs and prayers resonate with our own experiences, reminding us that we are not alone in our struggles. They also model a way of pouring out our anxious thoughts before God, interspersed with reminders of His faithfulness and protection. Engaging with these texts can provide comfort and perspective, reminding us of the bigger picture and the steadfastness of God's presence.

Community is another vital aspect highlighted in the journey towards serenity. The New Testament letters frequently encourage believers to bear one another's burdens, to encourage and pray for each other. This mutual support is not only a source of comfort but also a means of experiencing God's peace through the love and care of others. In sharing our anxieties within a trusted community, we find a shared human experience that often brings relief and a sense of belonging.

Moreover, the concept of **thanksgiving** intertwined with prayer is significant in managing anxiety. This practice involves acknowledging the good amidst the turmoil, which can shift our focus from our worries to the blessings we often overlook. Cultivating a habit of gratitude helps to frame our circumstances in a new light, fostering a sense of hope and contentment even in the midst of challenges.

As we delve deeper into understanding anxiety through a faith-based lens, it becomes evident that the biblical approach is multifaceted, addressing the spiritual, emotional, and communal dimensions of our lives. This holistic perspective not only validates our feelings of anxiety but also provides a pathway towards peace that is rooted in a deep relationship with God, engagement with Scripture, the support of a faith community, and the practice of gratitude.

The practice of **reflective listening** to God's voice through His Word and creation further enriches our understanding and management of anxiety. This involves quieting our hearts and minds to discern God's guidance and comfort in our lives. It is in these moments of stillness that we often receive the clarity and peace we seek. Reflective listening can be fostered through meditative reading of Scripture, where we not only read the words but also allow them to read us, speaking into our situations with wisdom and peace.

Faith in action is another critical aspect of navigating anxiety with a faith-based perspective. James, the brother of Jesus, emphasizes that faith without works is dead. Applying this principle to our struggle with anxiety means actively trusting God's promises by taking steps of faith in our daily lives. This could involve challenging ourselves to step out of our comfort zones, trusting that God's strength is made perfect in our weakness. Such actions, though often small, can significantly impact our sense of empowerment and reliance on God.

The role of **worship and praise** in combating anxiety cannot be overstated. As we lift our voices in praise, our focus shifts from our problems to the greatness of God. This act of worship is a powerful weapon against anxiety, as it realigns our perspective, reminding us of God's sovereignty and our identity as His beloved children. Whether through music, prayer, or reflection on God's attributes, worship is a vital practice for instilling peace in our hearts.

Fostering resilience through scriptural promises is crucial for enduring life's trials with peace. The Bible is rich with assurances of God's presence and help in times of trouble. Clinging to these promises helps to build a spiritual resilience that can withstand the storms of life. This resilience is cultivated through regular engagement with Scripture, memorization of key verses, and recalling God's faithfulness in past situations.

Service and giving also play a role in managing anxiety from a faith-based perspective. By focusing on the needs of others, we often find our own burdens lightened. Jesus modeled this principle through His life of service, teaching us that there is great joy and peace in giving of ourselves. Engaging in acts of kindness and service can shift our focus from our anxieties to the joy of blessing others, reflecting the love of Christ in tangible ways.

In conclusion, managing anxiety through a faith-based lens involves a comprehensive approach that includes prayer, engagement with Scripture, community support, thanksgiving, reflective listening, faith in action, worship and praise, fostering resilience, and service. Each of these practices offers a unique contribution to our journey towards peace, grounding us in the truth of God's Word and His unchanging character. As we incorporate these disciplines into our lives, we find not only relief from anxiety but also a deeper, more joyous relationship with God.

Recognizing God's Presence in Struggles

In the midst of our daily struggles, it's easy to feel overwhelmed and disconnected from God's presence. However, the Bible assures us that God is always with us, offering strength, comfort, and guidance through every challenge we face. To truly recognize and lean into this divine support, it's essential to cultivate practices that keep us attuned to God's active involvement in our lives.

Prayer is a fundamental way to connect with God amidst our daily challenges. It allows us to voice our concerns, fears, and needs, creating a space for God to comfort and guide us. By setting aside specific times for prayer each day, we can ensure that we are regularly seeking God's presence and allowing Him to influence our thoughts and actions. This consistent communication is key to recognizing God's hand at work in our lives.

Scripture reading offers another powerful avenue for encountering God in our struggles. The Bible is filled with stories of individuals who faced immense challenges yet found strength and hope in God. By immersing ourselves in these stories, we can draw parallels to our own situations and be reminded of God's faithfulness across the ages.

Regularly engaging with Scripture also allows God's Word to shape our understanding and response to the trials we encounter.

Worship in times of difficulty can be particularly transformative. Singing praises to God, even when our hearts are heavy, shifts our focus from our problems to God's greatness and love. This act of faith can break down walls of despair and open our hearts to God's peace and comfort. Whether through music, art, or another form of expression, worship is a vital practice for maintaining awareness of God's presence in our lives.

Community involvement plays a crucial role in recognizing God's work in our struggles. Sharing our burdens with fellow believers not only provides practical and emotional support but also offers a wider perspective on how God is moving within our community. Witnessing God's faithfulness in the lives of others can strengthen our own faith and remind us that we are not alone in our challenges.

Gratitude is a powerful tool for acknowledging God's presence in our daily struggles. By intentionally reflecting on the blessings in our lives, even during difficult times, we cultivate a mindset that looks for God's goodness and provision. Keeping a gratitude journal or simply taking time each day to reflect on what we're thankful for can help us to see God's hand in every situation, encouraging us to trust in His care and provision.

Meditation and reflection on God's promises can also anchor us in His presence. Setting aside time to quietly contemplate God's character and promises can calm our anxious minds and reorient our hearts towards His peace. This practice helps us to internalize the truth of God's Word, making it a source of strength and guidance in our daily lives.

By integrating these practices into our routine, we open ourselves up to recognizing God's presence in every aspect of our lives. As we pray, engage with Scripture, worship, connect with our community, express gratitude, and meditate on God's promises, we become more attuned to the ways God is working in and through our struggles. This awareness brings a deep sense of comfort and assurance, reinforcing our faith and providing a solid foundation of peace amidst the challenges of daily life.

3 Exercises for Peace in Scripture

Exercise 1: Reflective Scripture Journaling

Objective: To deepen your understanding and personal connection with scripture, using reflective journaling as a tool to explore your thoughts, feelings, and the presence of God in your life, fostering a sense of peace and serenity.

Step-by-step instructions:

1. **Select a Quiet Time and Place:** Choose a time and location where you won't be disturbed. Early morning or late evening can be ideal times when the house is quiet. Ensure your space is comfortable and inviting, perhaps with a comfortable chair and soft lighting.

2. **Gather Your Materials:** You will need a journal or notebook dedicated to this purpose, a pen, and your Bible. You may also want to have a cup of tea or coffee to create a comforting ritual around your journaling practice.

3. **Begin with Prayer:** Start your session with a short prayer, asking God to open your heart and mind to the insights He wishes to reveal to you through His Word. Request clarity, understanding, and a peaceful heart as you delve into scripture.

4. **Choose a Passage of Scripture:** If you're following a Bible reading plan, you may already have a passage for the day. Otherwise, choose a verse or passage that speaks to the theme of serenity, peace, or trust in God. Psalms, Proverbs, the Gospels, and Paul's letters are excellent sources of comforting and instructive scripture.

5. **Read the Scripture Slowly:** Read the selected passage slowly, at least three times. The first time, simply familiarize yourself with the text. The second time, pay attention to any words or phrases that stand out to you. The third time, consider how the passage relates to your current life circumstances.

6. **Reflect and Write:** Reflect on the passage and how it speaks to your heart. Start writing in your journal. You can write your thoughts, feelings, any words or phrases that

stood out to you, and why they might be significant. Consider how the scripture can apply to your life, any actions you might take, or how it might change your perspective on current challenges.

7. **Write a Prayer:** After reflecting on the passage and its personal implications, write a prayer in your journal. This prayer can be one of thanksgiving, confession, or petition, based on the reflections you've just penned down. Ask for God's guidance in applying the scripture's lessons to your life.

8. **Close in Silence:** After you've finished writing, spend a few moments in silence, sitting with the feelings and thoughts that arose during your journaling. This is a time to listen for God's still, small voice and to feel His peace enveloping you.

9. **Review Regularly:** Make a habit of reviewing your journal entries regularly, perhaps once a month or at the end of a notebook. This can help you see patterns in your spiritual journey, recognize answered prayers, and observe how your understanding and application of scripture have grown over time.

Remember, there is no right or wrong way to engage in reflective scripture journaling. The goal is to deepen your relationship with God; understand His Word better, and find peace and serenity through His promises.

Exercise 2: Guided Scripture Meditation

Objective: To deepen your connection with God and find peace through focused meditation on Scripture. This exercise aims to help you slow down, reflect on God's Word, and internalize its meaning for your life, fostering a sense of serenity and trust.

Step-by-step instructions:

1. **Choose a Quiet Space:** Find a quiet, comfortable place where you won't be disturbed. This could be a cozy corner of your home, a peaceful spot in your garden, or anywhere you feel at ease and free from distractions.

2. **Select a Scripture Passage:** Choose a passage that speaks to peace, trust, or God's promises. If you're unsure where to start, consider Philippians 4:6-7, Matthew 6:25-34, or Psalm 23. Write it down in a journal or have your Bible open to this passage.

3. **Prepare Your Heart:** Take a few deep breaths to center yourself. Pray for openness and ask God to speak to you through His Word. Express your desire to learn and find peace in His presence.

4. **Read the Scripture Aloud:** Read the chosen passage aloud slowly. Pay attention to each word and phrase. Notice any words or phrases that stand out to you.

5. **Reflect Quietly:** Close your eyes and meditate on the passage. Think about what it means to you personally. Consider how it applies to your current life situation. If your mind wanders, gently bring it back to the scripture or a specific word or phrase that struck you.

6. **Personalize the Scripture:** Imagine God speaking the words directly to you. Replace any general pronouns with your name to make it more personal. For example, "For God so loved the world" becomes "For God so loved [Your Name]."

7. **Write Your Reflections:** Open your eyes and jot down any thoughts, feelings, or insights that came to you during your meditation. Reflect on how this scripture can impact your daily life and how it can help you find peace.

8. **Pray and Surrender:** Conclude your meditation with a prayer. Thank God for His Word and the peace it brings. Surrender your worries and anxieties to Him, and ask for His guidance and strength to apply the scripture in your life.

9. **Practice Regularly:** Incorporate this guided scripture meditation into your daily or weekly routine. Over time, you'll notice a deeper sense of peace and serenity as you continue to meditate on God's promises and presence in your life.

Exercise 3: Scripture-Based Affirmations

Objective: To create and practice daily affirmations based on scripture, reinforcing the truth of God's word in your life and combating anxiety with faith.

Step-by-step instructions:

1. **Select Scripture Verses:** Begin by choosing five scripture verses that resonate deeply with you and address your specific fears or anxieties. Look for verses that affirm God's love, protection, and strength.

2. **Write Personalized Affirmations:** Transform each verse into a first-person affirmation. For example, if you chose Philippians 4:13, "I can do all things through Christ who strengthens me," becomes "I am empowered by Christ to overcome any challenge I face."

3. **Incorporate Relevant Life Contexts:** For each affirmation, write a brief sentence about how this truth applies to your current life situation, challenges, or anxieties. This step personalizes the affirmation, making it more impactful.

4. **Design Your Affirmation Cards:** On small cards or pieces of paper, neatly write down each scripture-based affirmation along with its application to your life. Decorate or color these cards in a way that brings you joy and makes them visually appealing.

5. **Establish a Daily Affirmation Routine:** Choose a time each day to read your affirmations aloud. Morning routines can be particularly effective as they set a positive tone for the day. However, choose a time that best fits into your daily schedule.

6. **Create a Visible Reminder:** Place your affirmation cards in locations where you will see them throughout the day. Consider spots like your bathroom mirror, car dashboard, or work desk. These visible reminders will help reinforce the affirmations as you go about your day.

7. **Reflect and Journal:** At the end of each week, spend some time reflecting on how these affirmations have impacted your thoughts and emotions. Journal any changes you've noticed in your anxiety levels or how you've seen God's promises manifest in your life.

8. **Adjust and Expand:** As you grow in this practice, feel free to adjust your affirmations or add new ones. The goal is to continuously embed God's truth into your daily life, transforming your mindset and reducing anxiety through faith.

Chapter 2: The Power of Prayer

Prayer, often perceived as a simple act of faith, holds profound power in mitigating anxiety and fostering a sense of peace that transcends human understanding. This spiritual discipline, when practiced consistently, becomes a lifeline, connecting the human heart to divine comfort and wisdom. In the midst of life's tumultuous waves, prayer anchors us to a steadfast hope and reassurance found only in the presence of our Creator. It is here, in the quiet communion with God, that the burdens of anxiety can be lifted and replaced with a serenity that is not easily shaken by the world's uncertainties.

The Scriptures offer numerous examples of individuals who turned to prayer in their moments of distress, demonstrating its effectiveness in calming the troubled mind. For instance, the Psalms are filled with David's earnest pleas and heartfelt prayers during times of fear and despair. His experiences teach us that bringing our anxieties before God is not only an act of obedience but also a profound source of comfort and strength. David's prayers often began with expressions of anguish but transitioned into declarations of trust and praise, highlighting the transformative power of prayer in shifting one's focus from anxiety to assurance.

To engage in prayer effectively, especially in the context of overcoming anxiety, it is essential to approach it with sincerity and openness, laying bare our fears and worries without reservation. This level of vulnerability fosters an intimate relationship with God, where we can receive His peace and guidance. Moreover, incorporating specific elements into our prayer life can enhance its impact on our mental and emotional well-being. These elements include:

1. **Thanksgiving**: Beginning our prayers with gratitude shifts our perspective from our problems to the blessings in our lives, reminding us of God's faithfulness and provision.
2. **Petition**: Candidly presenting our needs and concerns to God, trusting in His power to provide and His wisdom to ordain what is best for us.
3. **Intercession**: Praying for others not only cultivates empathy and compassion but also helps to alleviate our own anxieties as we focus on the needs of those around us.

4. **Praise**: Worshiping God for who He is, independent of our circumstances, realigns our hearts to His sovereignty and goodness, instilling peace within us.

Incorporating scripture into our prayers is another powerful practice. Praying God's Word back to Him not only reinforces our faith in His promises but also embeds these truths deeply within our hearts, serving as an antidote to fear and anxiety. Scriptures such as Philippians 4:6-7, which urges us not to be anxious about anything but to present our requests to God with thanksgiving, can be particularly comforting. Praying through such passages reminds us of the peace God offers, a peace that guards our hearts and minds in Christ Jesus.

Furthermore, the discipline of silent prayer, or contemplative prayer, allows us to sit in God's presence, listening for His voice and guidance. In these moments of stillness, we can find clarity and peace that come from being attuned to the divine whisper, often drowned out by the noise of our hectic lives. This practice requires patience and persistence, as it involves quieting our minds and focusing our thoughts on God, but the inner tranquility it fosters is well worth the effort.

As we delve deeper into the power of prayer in overcoming anxiety, it becomes evident that this spiritual exercise is not a one-time act but a lifestyle of ongoing dialogue with God. Through prayer, we are invited into a relationship of dependence on and trust in our Creator, who cares deeply about our worries and seeks to envelop us in His peace. This chapter aims to explore further the multifaceted nature of prayer and its role in navigating the complexities of anxiety, offering practical steps and insights to harness its potential for healing and transformation.

The practice of **listening prayer** further deepens one's connection to God, especially in the context of anxiety. This form of prayer emphasizes the importance of pausing to hear God's response to our petitions and thanksgivings. It's a deliberate act of opening one's heart to divine wisdom, seeking not just to speak but to receive. By cultivating a posture of receptiveness, we become more attuned to the subtle ways in which God communicates His love and guidance. This may come through the Scriptures, the inner prompting of the Holy Spirit, or through the circumstances and people He places in our path. The key is to remain open and attentive, acknowledging that God's answers to our prayers may not always align with our expectations but are always for our ultimate good.

Corporate prayer, or praying with others, is another dimension that can significantly impact one's journey towards peace. Gathering with fellow believers to lift up communal and individual concerns to God not only fosters a sense of solidarity but also amplifies our faith. Jesus Himself promised that where two or three are gathered in His name, He is there among them (Matthew 18:20). This assurance highlights the power of collective prayer and its capacity to usher in God's peace and presence in a tangible way. Whether in a church setting, a small group, or even a virtual prayer meeting, joining with others in prayer strengthens our communal bonds and our personal faith, reminding us that we are not alone in our struggles.

Fasting and prayer introduce an aspect of physical discipline that can enhance spiritual clarity and focus, especially when dealing with anxiety. This practice, which involves abstaining from food or other comforts for a spiritual purpose, helps to humble the soul and draw us closer to God. Fasting is not about earning God's favor but about prioritizing our spiritual desires over our physical needs. It sharpens our awareness of God's voice and can break down barriers in our hearts that hinder the flow of His peace. When combined with prayer, fasting becomes a powerful tool for seeking divine intervention and gaining victory over the anxieties that plague us.

Prayer walks offer a unique opportunity to engage in prayer while immersing oneself in the beauty of God's creation. This practice involves walking through a natural setting or even a neighborhood, praying silently or aloud for the people, homes, and issues one encounters along the way. Prayer walks can be especially refreshing for the soul, as they allow for physical movement and engagement with the surrounding environment, which can be therapeutic in itself. They remind us of God's sovereignty over all aspects of our world and encourage us to entrust our anxieties to Him, step by step.

Journaling prayers is a method that combines the act of prayer with the reflective practice of writing. This can be particularly helpful for those who struggle to focus during prayer or who wish to keep a record of their conversations with God. Writing down prayers, concerns, and the insights received during prayer times serves as a tangible reminder of God's faithfulness in answering prayers. It also allows for a deeper exploration of one's thoughts and feelings, facilitating a more thorough release of anxieties to God.

Each of these practices, when integrated into one's daily routine, can significantly bolster the effectiveness of prayer in combating anxiety. They offer diverse approaches to connect with God, ensuring that individuals can find methods that resonate with their unique personalities and circumstances. The goal is not to follow a rigid formula but to cultivate a dynamic and responsive prayer life that adapts to the needs of the moment. By doing so, we open ourselves up to the peace that God promises, a peace that not only calms our anxieties but also transforms our hearts and minds.

Cultivating Daily Prayer Habits

To cultivate a habit of daily prayer, it's essential to first establish a dedicated time and space for this spiritual practice. In the midst of a bustling lifestyle, setting aside a specific moment each day for prayer can seem daunting. However, this intentional act of carving out time in one's schedule is a testament to the value placed on connecting with the Divine. Whether it's early in the morning before the day's responsibilities beckon or in the evening when the house has quieted down, consistency is key. The goal is to create a rhythm that integrates prayer seamlessly into daily life, making it as natural as breathing.

Creating a prayer space that is conducive to open, heartfelt conversation with God can significantly enhance this daily practice. This doesn't require an elaborate setup but simply a quiet corner free from distractions where one can focus wholly on the act of prayer. This space can be personalized with items that inspire spiritual reflection, such as a Bible, a journal, or even a candle. The physical act of entering this space can help shift one's mindset from the secular to the sacred, fostering a deeper engagement in prayer.

Incorporating scripture into daily prayer is a powerful way to connect with God's Word and promises. Scriptures can serve as a starting point for prayer, guiding the conversation and focusing the mind on God's attributes and faithfulness. This practice not only enriches one's spiritual life but also embeds God's Word into the heart, equipping believers with biblical truths to face the challenges of the day. By selecting a verse or passage to meditate on and pray about each day, individuals can find fresh insights and encouragement that fuel their faith journey.

Another aspect of cultivating a daily prayer habit is the practice of listening. Prayer is a two-way conversation, and developing the discipline to listen for God's voice is crucial. This can involve sitting in silence after speaking, being attentive to the thoughts and impressions that arise. It may also include asking God questions and pausing to consider any insights that come to mind. This practice of listening fosters a deeper relationship with God, where prayer becomes not just a monologue but a dialogue.

Engagement with prayer partners or small groups can also be a meaningful way to deepen one's prayer life. Sharing prayer requests and committing to pray for one another creates a sense of community and accountability. It's encouraging to know others are praying with and for you, and such connections can strengthen one's commitment to daily prayer. This communal aspect of prayer mirrors the early church's practices and underscores the importance of fellowship in the believer's life.

Journaling prayers is another method that can enhance one's daily prayer practice. Writing down prayers, thoughts, and any responses felt during prayer time serves as a tangible record of one's spiritual journey. It allows for reflection on how God has answered prayers over time, which can be a significant faith booster during challenging periods. The act of writing can also help to focus one's thoughts and prayers, making the time spent in prayer more intentional and meaningful.

In the process of establishing a daily prayer habit, it's important to approach each day with grace and flexibility. Some days, prayer might be a lengthy, immersive experience, while on others, it might be brief but sincere check-ins with God throughout the day. The emphasis should be on the quality of the connection rather than the quantity of time spent. What matters most is the commitment to daily turn one's focus to God, inviting His presence into every aspect of life.

To further enrich the practice of daily prayer, incorporating specific themes or focuses can bring a new depth to one's spiritual routine. For instance, dedicating each day of the week to a particular prayer theme—such as gratitude on Mondays, intercession for others on Tuesdays, personal guidance on Wednesdays, etc.—can provide structure and variety, ensuring that prayer life remains vibrant and comprehensive. This approach not only covers a broad spectrum of prayer needs but also keeps the practice fresh and engaging.

The use of prayer aids, such as devotional books, prayer apps, or even music, can also play a significant role in enhancing one's daily communion with God. Devotionals provide daily scripture readings and reflections that can spark prayerful dialogue with God. Prayer apps might offer reminders to pray or guide users through themed prayers, making it easier to maintain consistency even on busy days. Music, particularly worship music, can help in setting a reverent atmosphere, opening the heart to receive and respond to God's presence.

Embracing the practice of gratitude within daily prayer is another transformative element. Starting or ending each prayer session by listing things one is thankful for shifts the focus from life's difficulties to its blessings, cultivating a heart of contentment and trust in God's provision. This habit not only enriches one's prayer life but also positively impacts one's overall outlook on life.

The integration of fasting with prayer at certain times can deepen one's spiritual discipline and focus. Fasting, whether from food, social media, or other distractions, creates additional space for prayer and reflection, heightening one's sensitivity to God's voice and presence. Even short periods of fasting can significantly enhance the intensity and sincerity of one's prayers, drawing the believer into a closer relationship with God.

Adopting the practice of praying Scripture back to God is a powerful way to align one's prayers with God's will. This involves selecting a passage of Scripture and using it as the basis for one's prayer, personalizing the words and applying them to one's life or the lives of others. This method not only deepens one's understanding of Scripture but also ensures that prayers are rooted in biblical truth.

Finally, remaining open to the Holy Spirit's leading in prayer is essential for a dynamic and responsive prayer life. This might mean being flexible with one's prayer schedule or content, allowing the Spirit to guide the focus of prayer based on immediate needs or promptings. Such sensitivity can lead to powerful moments of intercession and insight, making prayer a truly living and active dialogue with God.

Incorporating these practices into one's daily routine can transform prayer from a static, one-dimensional ritual into a rich, multifaceted dialogue with God. The key is to approach prayer with intentionality and openness, allowing it to evolve and adapt over time. By doing so, believers can ensure that their daily prayer habit remains a vital and nourishing part of their spiritual journey, fostering a deeper connection with God and a more resilient faith.

Thanksgiving and Praise in Healing

The act of **thanksgiving** and **praise** plays a pivotal role in the healing process, especially when dealing with anxiety. These practices not only shift our focus from our worries to God's omnipotence but also reinforce our faith, reminding us of His unending love and mercy. Engaging in thanksgiving allows us to recount God's faithfulness in past circumstances, providing us with the assurance that He is with us in our current struggles. Praise, on the other hand, elevates our spirit and aligns our heart with God's, enabling us to see our situations from His perspective.

To incorporate thanksgiving and praise into our daily routine, consider these specific actions:

- **Start each day with a declaration of gratitude.** Before even getting out of bed, think of three things you are thankful for. These can be as simple as the comfort of your bed or as profound as the gift of salvation. This practice sets a positive tone for the day, directing your thoughts towards God's blessings rather than the day's challenges.

- **Keep a gratitude journal.** Make it a habit to write down at least one thing you are grateful for each day. Over time, this journal will become a tangible reminder of God's goodness, encouraging you during times of doubt and anxiety.

- **Incorporate praise into your prayer life.** As you pray, include moments where you solely focus on praising God for who He is. Use Psalms as a guide for your praise, acknowledging God's attributes such as His wisdom, strength, and love.

- **Create a playlist of worship music.** Music has the power to uplift our spirits and shift our focus. Compile a list of your favorite worship songs that highlight God's goodness and faithfulness. Listen to this playlist during your commute, exercise, or household chores to fill your mind with uplifting truths.

- **Turn worries into worship.** When anxious thoughts begin to surface, consciously choose to praise God instead. This could mean verbally declaring truths about God's character or singing a worship song that speaks to your situation. This act of worship in the face of worry can break the cycle of anxiety, bringing peace to your heart.

- **Share testimonies of thankfulness.** In conversations with friends, family, or small group members, share stories of how you've seen God work in your life. These testimonies not only encourage others but also strengthen your own faith as you recall God's faithfulness.

- **Reflect on God's creation.** Spend time in nature, observing the beauty and intricacy of the world God has made. This practice can inspire awe and gratitude, drawing you into a posture of praise.

- **Practice the presence of God.** Throughout your day, pause to acknowledge God's presence with you. Offer up short prayers of thanks for His nearness and sovereignty over your life. This constant communication cultivates a heart of gratitude and worship.

By intentionally practicing thanksgiving and praise, we open our hearts to receive God's peace and healing. These acts of faith remind us of our dependence on God and His sufficiency to meet our every need. As we focus on God's character and deeds, we find our anxiety replaced with a profound sense of peace and trust in His providential care. Through thanksgiving and praise, we not only experience healing for our own hearts but also become beacons of God's light and love to those around us, demonstrating the transformative power of living a life anchored in gratitude and worship.

Exercises to Deepen Your Prayer Life

Exercise 4: Prayerful Visualization Techniques

Objective: This exercise aims to deepen your prayer life by integrating visualization techniques, helping you to envision God's presence and promises in your life, thereby enhancing your spiritual connection and reducing anxiety.

Step-by-step instructions:

1. **Select a Scripture Passage:** Choose a passage from the Bible that speaks to God's promises, protection, or love. This could be a verse that you find comforting or one that you wish to explore more deeply.

2. **Find a Quiet Space:** Locate a peaceful area where you will not be disturbed. This could be a favorite chair in your home, a spot in your garden, or any place that you associate with tranquility and prayer.

3. **Prepare Your Heart and Mind:** Begin with a few deep breaths to center yourself. Pray for openness and receptivity to God's word, asking Him to speak to you through this exercise.

4. **Read the Scripture Aloud:** Slowly read the selected scripture passage aloud. Pay attention to each word and phrase, allowing the Holy Spirit to highlight elements of the text that are meant for you in this moment.

5. **Visualize the Scene:** Close your eyes and imagine the scene or promise described in the scripture. If the passage speaks of God's protection, for example, visualize yourself enveloped in God's loving arms. Use all your senses to immerse yourself in the visualization – what do you see, hear, feel?

6. **Place Yourself in the Presence of God:** As you visualize, see yourself standing or sitting in God's presence. Imagine His light surrounding you, His peace filling the space. Feel His love and assurance wash over you.

7. **Speak to God:** In this visualized space, talk to God. Share your worries, fears, and thanksgivings. Use the scripture as a starting point for your conversation. If the verse is a promise, thank Him for it; if it's a command, ask for His help to obey.

8. **Listen for God's Response:** After you've spoken, remain in silence and openness, listening for God's voice. He may speak through thoughts, feelings, or even further visualization. Trust that He is communicating with you.

9. **Write Down Your Experience:** Once you feel the exercise is complete, write down what you experienced, including any insights, emotions, or messages you received. Reflect on how this visualization has deepened your understanding of the scripture and your relationship with God.

10. **Integrate the Visualization into Daily Life:** Throughout your day, recall the visualization whenever you need a reminder of God's promises or presence. This practice can help carry the peace and assurance from your prayer time into your daily activities.

11. **Repeat Regularly:** Engage in this exercise with different scripture passages as often as you can, ideally making it a regular part of your prayer life. Each session will deepen your spiritual connection and enhance your sense of serenity.

Chapter 3: Trusting God's Plan

In the pursuit of serenity, a significant barrier many face is the deeply ingrained desire to maintain control over every aspect of our lives. This chapter delves into the liberating process of trusting in God's plan, which invites us to release our grip on the reins of life and surrender our fears and anxieties to a higher power. The act of letting go is not a passive resignation but an active engagement in faith, acknowledging that while we may not understand the full picture, we can trust in God's omniscience and benevolence.

The Scriptures provide numerous instances where individuals faced seemingly insurmountable challenges, yet found peace and resolution by placing their trust in God. Consider the story of Abraham, called to leave everything familiar behind on a promise, or Moses, leading a nation to freedom against all odds. These narratives are not just historical accounts but are alive with lessons on the power of surrendering control.

In practical terms, letting go requires a daily commitment to trust, prayer, and reflection. It involves recognizing the moments when our thoughts and actions are driven by fear or a desire for control and consciously choosing to place those concerns in God's hands. This process may start with small, everyday worries but can gradually encompass larger areas of our lives, including our plans, relationships, and dreams.

One of the first steps in learning to let go is identifying the areas of our life where we seek control. This could range from micro-managing daily tasks to overarching concerns about our career path, family well-being, or health issues. Acknowledging these areas is crucial, as it sets the stage for understanding our underlying fears and anxieties. It's often our deepest insecurities that drive us to cling to control, believing that if we can just manage every detail, we can protect ourselves and our loved ones from harm.

However, this relentless pursuit of control not only leads to increased anxiety but also distances us from the peace and assurance found in trusting God's plan. By surrendering our fears to God, we make room for His peace to fill our hearts, a peace that surpasses all understanding, as described in Philippians 4:7. This divine peace does not mean the absence of trouble but signifies a confidence and rest in God's sovereignty, regardless of life's circumstances.

To cultivate this trust, engaging in daily practices that reinforce our reliance on God is beneficial. Prayer, not as a wish list to God but as a conversation with a loving Father, becomes a powerful tool in surrendering control. Through prayer, we express our fears, desires, and hopes, laying them at God's feet and inviting His guidance and wisdom into our lives. Additionally, meditating on Scriptures that affirm God's promises and care can fortify our hearts against the impulse to take back control. Verses like Proverbs 3:5-6, which urges us to trust in the Lord with all our heart and lean not on our own understanding, can be a balm to the anxious mind striving for control.

As we journey through this process of letting go and trusting God's plan, it's essential to remember that setbacks and moments of doubt are part of the human experience. The key is not to berate ourselves in these moments but to gently redirect our focus to God's faithfulness and love. Each act of surrender, no matter how small, is a step towards a deeper relationship with God and a life characterized by lasting serenity.

Engaging in reflective scripture journaling can be a transformative exercise for those learning to trust in God's plan. By writing down thoughts and reflections on passages that speak to surrender and trust, individuals create a personal dialogue with God. This practice not only allows for a deeper understanding of His promises but also serves as a tangible reminder of His faithfulness in past situations. Reflective journaling can become a sanctuary where fears and worries are exchanged for comfort and assurance in God's providence.

Guided scripture meditation further complements the journey towards letting go. By focusing on God's Word and allowing its truth to permeate our hearts and minds, we can experience a shift from anxiety to peace. This form of meditation invites the Holy Spirit to speak into our lives, revealing areas where we need to release control and trust more deeply in God's guidance. It's in these moments of quiet reflection that many find the strength to surrender their deepest fears.

Scripture-based affirmations act as daily reminders of God's sovereignty and our identity in Him. Phrases like "I am a child of God, led by His wisdom" or "I trust in the Lord's plans, not my own" can be powerful tools in reshaping our thought patterns. By declaring these truths over our lives, we actively choose faith over fear and trust over control. These affirmations serve as anchors, keeping us grounded in God's truth amid life's storms.

The importance of prayer in this process cannot be overstated. Prayerful visualization techniques, where individuals imagine handing over their worries to God, can be particularly effective. This practice not only helps in releasing specific concerns but also in cultivating a deeper sense of trust in God's care for every aspect of our lives. Visualizing our fears as burdens being lifted off our shoulders can provide a profound sense of relief and reinforce our confidence in God's loving oversight.

Community and fellowship play a crucial role in supporting individuals on their journey to trust in God's plan. Sharing experiences, struggles, and victories with others who are also learning to let go can be incredibly affirming. It's within the context of a supportive faith community that individuals can find encouragement, understanding, and prayerful support. Moreover, witnessing how others navigate their journey of trust can offer valuable insights and inspiration.

Gratitude practice, finally, shifts our focus from what we cannot control to the blessings we currently have. By cultivating an attitude of thankfulness, even in challenging circumstances, we open our hearts to recognize God's goodness and provision. This shift in perspective is vital for maintaining peace and serenity, as it reminds us of God's faithfulness and the countless ways He works in our lives, often beyond our understanding.

In embracing these practices, individuals embark on a transformative journey from a life marked by anxiety and the need for control to one of peace and trust in God's unchanging promises. Each step taken in faith, each practice incorporated into daily life, builds a foundation for lasting serenity that withstands the uncertainties of the world. Through prayer, reflection, and community, we learn to see our lives through the lens of God's sovereignty, embracing each day with confidence in His unfailing love and care.

Identifying Areas We Try to Control

Once we have pinpointed the domains in our lives where we exert excessive control, the next step involves understanding the root causes of this behavior. Often, our compulsion to manage every detail stems from underlying fears and insecurities. These might include the fear of failure, the dread of uncertainty, or anxiety about being perceived as inadequate. By acknowledging these fears, we can begin to address them directly, rather than allowing them to drive our need for control.

Developing awareness of our control tendencies is crucial. This can be achieved through daily reflection and mindfulness practices. By setting aside time each day to contemplate our actions and motivations, we can start to recognize patterns of behavior that are driven by an underlying need for control. This self-awareness is the first step toward change.

Prayer and Scripture offer profound sources of strength and guidance in this process. By turning to prayer, we can seek God's wisdom and ask for His help in relinquishing our need for control. Scripture, too, provides countless examples of individuals who faced their fears and learned to trust in God's plan. Meditating on these passages can inspire us to do the same.

Engaging in community with fellow believers can also provide support and encouragement. Sharing our struggles and victories with others who understand the journey can be incredibly affirming. It reminds us that we are not alone in our efforts to trust more deeply in God's plan.

To effectively **surrender our need for control**, it's helpful to practice specific **spiritual disciplines**. These might include:

1. **Prayerful Surrender**: Each day, dedicate time to pray specifically about the areas of life you struggle to release control over. Use this time to consciously hand these concerns over to God, affirming your trust in His care.

2. **Scripture Memorization**: Commit to memory verses that speak to the issue of control and trust. Reciting these verses during moments of stress or anxiety can help redirect your thoughts and reinforce your commitment to trust in God.

3. **Gratitude Journaling**: Make it a daily habit to jot down things you are thankful for. This practice shifts your focus from worries and the need to control to recognizing God's ongoing provision and presence in your life.

4. **Spiritual Accountability**: Partner with a trusted friend or mentor with whom you can share your journey toward trusting God more fully. This relationship can provide encouragement, prayer support, and gentle reminders of your commitment to let go of control.

5. **Service and Giving**: Engaging in acts of service and generosity can also help shift our focus away from our own desires for control. By serving others, we practice putting our trust in God to use our efforts for His purposes, which can be incredibly freeing.

Each of these practices offers a way to practically apply our desire to trust God more fully and to relinquish our grip on the areas of life we try to control. Through prayer, reflection, community, and action, we can move toward a deeper reliance on God's plan, experiencing the peace and serenity that comes from living a life surrendered to His will.

Surrendering Our Fears to God

In the act of surrendering our fears to God, it's vital to approach Him with honesty and vulnerability. This means laying bare our deepest worries, not in a manner of simply listing our troubles, but engaging in a heartfelt dialogue where we acknowledge our inability to solve these issues on our own. It's in this space of openness that we truly begin to experience the comforting embrace of God's love, a love that reassures us of His omnipotent presence in our lives, capable of transcending any obstacle we might face.

Developing a routine of surrender becomes a cornerstone of this process. Each morning, before the day's responsibilities demand our attention, dedicating a moment to speak with God about the upcoming day can set a foundation of peace. This conversation might include acknowledging the tasks that cause anxiety, expressing our desire for control, and actively deciding to trust God with these details. Similarly, ending the day with a reflective prayer, reviewing moments where we successfully surrendered and areas where we struggled, helps in recognizing God's hand in our daily lives.

Scriptural engagement plays a crucial role in reinforcing our commitment to trust God. By immersing ourselves in the stories of biblical figures who faced their fears with faith, we find encouragement and practical insights. For instance, the tale of David facing Goliath, armed with nothing but his faith in God, serves as a powerful reminder of the victory that awaits us when we place our trust in divine strength rather than our own.

Creating a support system within a faith community offers additional strength and perspective. Engaging in small group discussions or prayer meetings where members share their experiences of surrendering control can be incredibly uplifting. These gatherings provide a platform for collective prayer, where the burdens of each individual are lifted by the group's intercessory prayers, fostering a sense of communal trust in God's plan.

Practical exercises to facilitate the surrender of control include:
1. **Writing letters to God**: This exercise involves penning down our fears, frustrations, and desires, and then symbolically handing them over to God by placing them in a designated box or journal. This act serves as a physical representation of entrusting our concerns to Him.

2. **Visualization**: Taking time to visualize our worries being transferred from our hands into God's can be a powerful mental exercise in relinquishing control. This practice can be enhanced through guided imagery sessions, either individually or within a group setting, focusing on the peace and lightness that comes from surrendering our burdens.

3. **Committing Scripture to memory**: Selecting verses that speak directly to the concept of trust and surrender, such as Isaiah 41:10, and committing them to memory. This practice equips us with immediate reminders of God's promises when anxiety or the need to control arises.

4. **Engaging in acts of service**: Focusing on the needs of others allows us to step outside of our own concerns and, in doing so, often provides a fresh perspective on our own situations. Service acts as a reminder of our role in God's larger plan, one that is interconnected with the lives of others and guided by His hand.

5. **Practicing gratitude**: Maintaining a daily gratitude journal where we note not just the blessings we've received but also the challenges, viewing them as opportunities for growth and increased reliance on God. This shift in perspective is crucial for moving from a mindset of control to one of trust.

Through these practices, the act of surrendering our fears to God becomes less about a single moment of relinquishment and more about a continuous journey of deepening trust and faith. It's a journey marked by daily decisions to let go of our worries and embrace the peace that comes from believing in a God who is infinitely wise, loving, and capable of guiding us through every aspect of our lives. Engaging in this process not only alleviates our anxieties but also transforms our relationship with God, making it more intimate and rooted in trust. By consistently choosing to surrender our fears, we open ourselves to the profound peace and joy that come from living in alignment with God's will, a state of serenity that truly transcends all understanding.

5 Exercises on Trust and Surrender

Exercise 5: Trust-Building Prayer Practices

Objective: To cultivate a deeper trust in God through dedicated prayer practices that focus on surrendering control and embracing God's plan for our lives.

Step-by-step instructions:

1. **Prepare Your Environment:** Find a quiet, comfortable space where you won't be interrupted. This could be a special chair in your home, a spot in your garden, or any place that brings you peace.

2. **Gather Your Tools:** Bring your Bible, a notebook, and a pen. You may also want to have a comforting beverage, like tea or coffee, to help create a serene atmosphere.

3. **Start with Praise:** Begin your prayer time by praising God for who He is and acknowledging His sovereignty and goodness. This can be done through singing, reading a Psalm aloud, or simply speaking words of adoration.

4. **Read a Passage on Trust:** Choose a scripture passage that focuses on trust, such as Proverbs 3:5-6, and meditate on it. Read the passage several times, allowing the words to sink deeply into your heart.

5. **Reflect on Areas of Control:** Think about areas of your life where you struggle to relinquish control to God. Write these down in your notebook as they come to mind.

6. **Pray for Surrender:** For each area you've listed, pray specifically for the ability to surrender it to God. Ask for His guidance, and express your desire to trust Him more fully in these aspects of your life.

7. **Visualize Letting Go:** For each area of control, visualize yourself physically handing it over to God. Imagine placing it in His hands and feel the weight lifting off your shoulders as you do so.

8. **Affirm Your Trust:** Create a personal affirmation of trust based on scripture, such as "I trust in the Lord with all my heart, and I lean not on my own understanding." Repeat this affirmation aloud, slowly, and with conviction.

9. **Listen for God's Voice:** Spend a few moments in silence, listening for what God might be saying to you. Be open to any thoughts, feelings, or impressions that come during this time.

10. **Journal Your Experience:** Write down any insights or messages you received during your prayer time. Reflect on how this exercise has impacted your ability to trust in God.

11. **Commit to Daily Trust:** Decide on one small action you can take each day to demonstrate your trust in God. Write this down and commit to doing it daily.

12. **Close in Thanksgiving:** End your prayer time by thanking God for His presence and for any insights you've gained. Trust that He is at work in your life, even in ways you may not yet see.

Chapter 4: The Strength in Stillness

In the realm of spiritual growth and the pursuit of serenity, the practice of **listening** stands as a cornerstone. It is through the cultivation of stillness that one can truly hear the whisper of God's voice, guiding, comforting, and teaching. This section delves into the transformative exercises designed to enhance our ability to listen deeply, not only to God but also to the inner workings of our own hearts, where His spirit resides.

Deep Breathing for Inner Calm: Begin by finding a quiet space where interruptions are unlikely. Sit comfortably, close your eyes, and focus on your breathing. Inhale deeply through your nose, allowing your abdomen to expand fully, then exhale slowly through your mouth. With each breath, envision yourself drawing closer to God's presence. This exercise serves as a preparatory step, calming the mind and body to create a conducive environment for listening.

Mindful Listening to Nature: Nature, in its vast beauty and complexity, reflects the glory of the Creator. Spend time outdoors, in a garden, park, or any natural setting where the sounds of life abound. As you walk or sit quietly, pay attention to the sounds around you - the rustling of leaves, the chirping of birds, the gentle flow of water. Each sound is a testament to God's creativity and a reminder of His presence in the natural world. This practice not only heightens our awareness of our surroundings but also tunes our hearts to the divine rhythm of creation.

Silent Reflection Walk: Choose a path or area where you can walk safely without the need for conversation or interaction with others. As you walk, let go of the urge to fill the silence with thoughts or prayers. Instead, allow your mind to settle on the sensation of movement, the rhythm of your steps, and the stillness within. This exercise is a form of moving meditation, where the act of walking in silence becomes a medium for hearing God's voice in the quiet moments.

Heartfelt Listening in Prayer: Prayer is often perceived as a one-way communication, where we do most of the talking. However, prayer also involves listening - being open and receptive to what God might be saying to us. After presenting your thoughts and requests to God, remain in a posture of silence and expectancy. You might not receive an immediate answer or any discernible message, but this practice cultivates a mindset of openness to divine guidance whenever and however it may come.

Engaging in these practices regularly can significantly enhance one's ability to listen and discern God's voice amid the noise and distractions of daily life. Each exercise is designed not only to quiet the external environment but also to still the inner turmoil that often prevents us from hearing clearly. As we grow in our listening skills, we become more attuned to the nuances of God's guidance, leading to a deeper, more intimate relationship with Him. This, in turn, fosters a sense of peace and serenity that permeates all areas of our lives, empowering us to navigate challenges with grace and confidence. Through the disciplined practice of listening, we open ourselves to the transformative power of God's word, allowing it to shape our thoughts, actions, and attitudes in accordance with His will.

The Importance of Silence

In this fast-paced era, where the buzz of technology and the clamor of daily obligations often drown out tranquility, the discipline of seeking silence becomes not just beneficial but essential for spiritual and emotional well-being. Silence, in its purest form, is a canvas for the divine, a sacred space where the voice of God can paint strokes of guidance, comfort, and wisdom. It is in these quiet moments that the soul finds its voice and the whispers of the Holy Spirit become audible. Cultivating an environment conducive to silence requires intentional actions and a conscious withdrawal from the cacophony that characterizes much of modern life. This might involve setting aside specific times and places where quiet can be ensured and distractions minimized. Creating such sanctuaries of silence within one's daily routine can serve as spiritual lifelines, places of refuge where the heart can commune with God without interruption.

The benefits of integrating periods of silence into one's life are manifold. Firstly, it allows for deeper meditation on scripture, enabling the words to sink into the heart and mind on a more profound level than is possible amidst noise and activity. This meditative practice not only enriches understanding but also embeds these divine promises into the fabric of one's being, providing strength and comfort in times of need. Secondly, silence fosters an enhanced awareness of God's presence. In the stillness, the subtle indicators of His involvement in our lives become more apparent, fostering a sense of connectedness and support that can carry one through the darkest valleys. Additionally, the practice of silence cultivates a spirit of listening, a crucial skill for anyone seeking to deepen their relationship with God. It is often through the quiet nudges and soft promptings that God directs paths and imparts wisdom, but these can easily be missed in the hustle and bustle of daily life.

To effectively incorporate silence into one's spiritual regimen, consider the following strategies:

1. Begin each day with a moment of silence, dedicating the first minutes upon waking to sit quietly in God's presence. This sets a tone of peace and purpose for the day ahead.

2. Schedule short "silence breaks" throughout the day. These can be as brief as five minutes but should be times devoted entirely to quiet reflection and prayer.

3. Make use of technology to create an atmosphere of silence. Apps that provide timed silence intervals or play soft, non-distracting sounds can help in carving out islands of tranquility in a sea of noise.

4. Engage in silent retreats, whether formally organized or self-directed. Dedicating larger blocks of time to silence and solitude can provide deeper spiritual renewal and insight.

5. Practice mindfulness and presence in daily activities, turning routine tasks into opportunities for silent communion with God. Washing dishes, walking, or even waiting in line can become sacred moments when approached with intentionality.

6. Finally, cultivate a mindset that values and seeks out silence. Recognizing the power of quiet to restore and rejuvenate the spirit is the first step in making it a non-negotiable part of one's life.

Incorporating these practices requires patience and persistence, as the pull of the world's noise is strong and constant. Yet, the rewards of persistently seeking silence are profound.

In the quiet, the soul finds rest, the mind gains clarity, and the heart draws closer to the divine. Silence becomes not just an absence of noise but a sanctuary for the spirit, a place where God's voice is clear and His presence palpable. Through the disciplined pursuit of silence, believers can navigate the challenges of life with a sense of peace and assurance that is rooted not in the circumstances of the world but in the unchanging nature of God's love and faithfulness.

Hearing God in Quiet Moments

The cultivation of an environment where one can discern the subtle messages from God requires a deliberate effort to minimize distractions and foster a mindset conducive to receiving. This deep listening goes beyond merely seeking answers or guidance; it encompasses a readiness to be transformed by what we hear. The art of discerning God's voice in the quiet moments hinges on several key practices, each designed to prepare the heart and mind for divine encounters.

Developing a Routine of Intentional Silence: Establish a daily practice of spending time in silence, free from the intrusions of the digital world and the demands of daily tasks. This could be early in the morning before the day begins or in the evening as a way to conclude the day's activities. The goal is to create a sacred space where your attention is fully devoted to being present with God, allowing His voice to become the focus of your meditation.

Scriptural Immersion with a Listening Heart: Approach your reading of the Scriptures not just as a study but as a conversation with God. Read slowly, reflectively, and expectantly, paying attention to any verse or phrase that seems to resonate more deeply. Pause at these moments, inviting God to speak into your heart through His Word. This practice, often referred to as Lectio Divina, transforms Scripture reading from a routine into a dynamic interaction with the Divine.

Journaling as a Form of Prayerful Dialogue: Keep a journal dedicated to your spiritual reflections and insights. Write down the thoughts and feelings that arise during your times of silence and Scripture reading. This can include questions you have for God, areas of your life where you need guidance, or simply reflections on what you feel God is communicating to you through His Word. Journaling can serve as a tangible record of your spiritual journey and a means of discerning patterns or themes in what God might be revealing to you over time.

Cultivating Patience and Openness: Recognize that hearing God's voice is not always instantaneous or clear-cut. It often requires patience and a willingness to remain open to His timing and methods of communication. This might mean that answers or guidance come gradually, through a variety of means—circumstances, conversations with others, a sense of peace about a decision, or a gradual change of heart about a particular matter.

Practicing the Presence of God in Daily Activities: Beyond dedicated times of silence and prayer, seek to cultivate an ongoing awareness of God's presence in all aspects of your life. This practice, known as "practicing the presence of God," involves acknowledging God's nearness in every moment and seeking to remain open to His guidance throughout the day. Whether you're engaged in work, spending time with family, or performing mundane tasks, invite God into those moments with the expectation that He can speak to you at any time.

By integrating these practices into your daily life, you create a fertile ground for hearing God's voice in the quiet moments. Each practice is a step towards deepening your relationship with God, enhancing your ability to discern His will, and transforming your spiritual journey into one marked by a continuous, intimate dialogue with the Divine. The key is consistency and a heartfelt desire to know God more fully, trusting that He is always speaking to those who are willing to listen.

4 Exercises for Stillness and Listening

Exercise 6: Deep Breathing for Inner Calm

Objective: To utilize deep breathing as a tool for achieving inner calm, enhancing your ability to listen to God in the stillness, and fostering a serene mind and spirit amidst the busyness of daily life.

Step-by-step instructions:

1. **Find a Quiet Space:** Choose a location where you can sit or lie down comfortably without interruptions. This could be a quiet room in your home, a secluded spot in your yard, or any place that feels peaceful to you.

2. **Set a Timer:** Use a timer to allocate a specific amount of time for this exercise. Starting with five minutes is a good benchmark, but feel free to adjust according to your comfort level.

3. **Adopt a Comfortable Posture:** Sit comfortably with your back straight but not stiff. If you prefer to lie down, ensure your body is aligned and relaxed. Place your hands on your knees or by your sides, palms facing up or down based on what feels most natural to you.

4. **Close Your Eyes:** Gently close your eyes to minimize external distractions. This will help you focus inward and become more aware of your breathing and the presence of God.

5. **Focus on Your Breath:** Begin to notice your natural breathing pattern without trying to change it. Pay attention to the rise and fall of your chest and the sensation of air moving in and out of your nostrils.

6. **Deepen Your Breaths:** Slowly start to deepen your breaths. Inhale slowly through your nose, allowing your stomach to expand, and then exhale slowly through your mouth or nose, whichever feels more comfortable. Aim for each inhale and exhale to last around six seconds.

7. **Visualize Peace:** As you breathe deeply, visualize God's peace filling your heart and mind with each inhale and any tension or anxiety leaving your body with each exhale. Imagine yourself in a place of absolute serenity in God's presence.

8. **Incorporate Scripture:** Select a verse that embodies God's peace and serenity, such as Philippians 4:7. Silently repeat this verse in your mind as you breathe in and out, allowing the words to anchor you in the truth of God's promise of peace.

9. **Return Gently:** When your timer signals the end of your session, gently open your eyes. Take a moment to sit quietly, acknowledging the presence of God with you and the calmness you've cultivated.

10. **Reflect and Journal:** After completing the exercise, spend a few minutes reflecting on the experience. Journal any thoughts, feelings, or insights that arose during your time of deep breathing. Note any differences in your level of calmness and serenity.

11. **Practice Regularly:** Commit to practicing this deep breathing exercise daily. Over time, you may increase the duration as you become more comfortable with the practice. Regular deep breathing in the presence of God can significantly enhance your sense of peace and ability to listen for His guidance in the stillness.

12. **Integrate Throughout Your Day:** Beyond your dedicated practice time, use deep breathing to center yourself in moments of stress or busyness. A few deep breaths can help you return to a state of calm and remind you of God's constant presence and peace.

Exercise 7: Mindful Listening to Nature

Objective: To enhance your sense of inner calm and deepen your connection with God by mindfully listening to the natural world, recognizing His presence in the simplicity and beauty of creation.

Step-by-step instructions:

1. **Choose Your Setting:** Find a quiet spot outdoors where you are surrounded by elements of nature. This could be a park, your backyard, or near a body of water. Ensure it's a place where you can sit undisturbed for a period of time.

2. **Prepare Yourself:** Before you begin, take a few deep breaths to center yourself. Offer a short prayer, inviting God to join you in this time of listening and to open your ears and heart to the sounds of His creation.

3. **Assume a Comfortable Position:** Sit or stand in a way that you can remain relaxed and alert. You may choose to close your eyes to enhance your auditory senses or keep them open to observe the natural beauty around you.

4. **Begin to Listen:** Focus on the sounds of nature around you. It might be the rustling of leaves, the chirping of birds, the babbling of a brook, or the wind whispering through the trees. Try to identify each sound individually at first.

5. **Deepen Your Listening:** After identifying individual sounds, expand your listening to encompass the entire symphony of natural sounds around you. Notice how all these sounds exist together in harmony.

6. **Reflect on God's Creation:** As you listen, ponder the incredible diversity and balance in God's creation. Think about how each element of nature has a role and purpose, reflecting God's intricate design and care.

7. **Identify God's Presence:** In the quiet of nature, seek to feel God's presence around you. Consider how the natural world is a gift and a reminder of His love and provision for all creatures.

8. **Pray in Response:** Offer prayers of thanksgiving and awe for the beauty of creation you are experiencing. Ask God to help you carry this sense of peace and mindfulness into your daily life, recognizing His presence in even the smallest details.

9. **Journal Your Experience:** After your time of listening, write down your reflections in a journal. Note any new insights about God's character revealed through nature, how you felt during the exercise, and any scripture that comes to mind.

10. **Commit to Mindful Listening Daily:** Set a goal to incorporate mindful listening into your daily routine, even if just for a few minutes. It can be as simple as listening to the rain, birds from your window, or the leaves rustling as you walk.

By regularly engaging in mindful listening to nature, you can develop a deeper appreciation for God's creation, fostering a greater sense of serenity and connection to the divine in your everyday life.

Exercise 8: Silent Reflection Walk

Objective: To cultivate inner calm and enhanced spiritual listening through a silent reflection walk, allowing the natural rhythm of walking and the serenity of nature to quiet the mind and foster a deeper connection with God.

Step-by-step instructions:

1. **Choose Your Setting:** Select a location that embodies tranquility and natural beauty, such as a park, forest trail, or quiet neighborhood path. Ensure it's a place where you can walk safely without the need for frequent stops or attention to traffic.

2. **Prepare Mentally and Spiritually:** Before beginning your walk, take a few moments to pray, asking God to walk with you and speak to your heart during this time. Set an intention to release your anxieties and listen for God's guidance.

3. **Leave Distractions Behind:** Ensure you're free from distractions. This means leaving your phone, music player, and other electronic devices behind, or at least turning them off to avoid interruptions.

4. **Begin with Deep Breathing:** Start your walk with a minute of deep breathing to center yourself. Inhale deeply through your nose, hold for a few seconds, and exhale slowly through your mouth. This helps to calm your mind and body, preparing you for reflective silence.

5. **Walk at a Leisurely Pace:** Maintain a slow, comfortable pace that allows you to fully absorb your surroundings without exerting yourself too much. The goal is not physical exercise but spiritual and emotional rejuvenation.

6. **Observe Your Surroundings:** As you walk, gently observe the beauty around you without labeling or judging. Notice the colors, textures, and sounds. Let the beauty of God's creation remind you of His presence and care.

7. **Practice Mindful Walking:** With each step, be mindful of your movement and the sensations in your body. Feel your feet touching the ground, the rhythm of your breath,

and the gentle movements of your limbs. This mindfulness can help bring you into the present moment, reducing stress and enhancing spiritual receptivity.

8. **Pause for Reflection:** Find a comfortable spot to pause midway through your walk. Sit quietly and reflect on any thoughts, feelings, or impressions that have arisen. Offer these reflections to God in silent prayer, seeking His will and direction.

9. **Return with Gratitude:** As you make your way back, focus on feelings of gratitude. Thank God for His creation, the insights received, and His constant presence in your life. This gratitude can shift your perspective, reducing anxiety and promoting peace.

10. **Journal Your Experience:** Once home, take a few minutes to journal about your experience. Write down any insights, emotions, or messages you felt during your walk. Reflecting on these can deepen your understanding and application of the exercise.

11. **Integrate into Regular Practice:** Aim to incorporate silent reflection walks into your routine, varying your settings and times to explore different aspects of stillness and listening to God. Regular practice can significantly enhance your sense of serenity and connection to the divine.

Exercise 9: Heartfelt Listening in Prayer

Objective: To deepen your spiritual connection and enhance inner peace through the practice of heartfelt listening in prayer, focusing on the presence and guidance of God.

Step-by-step instructions:

1. **Prepare Your Space:** Find a quiet, comfortable place where you won't be disturbed. This could be a favorite spot in your home where you feel at peace. Ensure the environment is conducive to focus and reflection.

2. **Gather Necessary Items:** Have your Bible, a journal, and a pen ready. You may also want to light a candle or have some soft instrumental music in the background to help set a serene atmosphere.

3. **Begin with Silence:** Sit quietly for a few minutes, taking deep breaths to calm your mind and body. Use this time to transition your focus inward and acknowledge God's presence.

4. **Invoke the Holy Spirit:** Pray for the Holy Spirit to guide your listening and prayer time. Ask for openness to hear what God wants to communicate to you.

5. **Read a Scripture Passage:** Select a passage from the Bible that speaks to your heart or pertains to an area of your life where you seek guidance. Read it slowly, multiple times, allowing the words to sink in.

6. **Reflect on the Passage:** Consider what message God might be imparting through the scripture. Ponder any words or phrases that stand out to you and what they mean in the context of your life.

7. **Enter into Heartfelt Prayer:** Share your thoughts, feelings, and desires with God in a conversational manner. Be honest and open, as if speaking with a trusted friend. This is your time to connect deeply with God, expressing gratitude, seeking forgiveness, and asking for guidance.

8. **Listen with Your Heart:** After you've shared with God, remain in silence, focusing on your heart. Listen for God's response. This may come as a sense of peace, an insight, or an inner knowing. Be patient and give God the space to speak.

9. **Journal Your Experience:** Write down any thoughts, feelings, or messages you believe you received from God. Reflect on how this exercise has impacted your relationship with Him and any steps you feel called to take moving forward.

10. **Close with Thankfulness:** End your prayer time by thanking God for His presence and the insights or peace you've received. Acknowledge His ongoing guidance and love in your life.

11. **Integrate Throughout Your Day:** Carry the essence of this heartfelt listening into your daily activities. When faced with decisions or moments of stress, pause to listen for God's guidance, remembering the peace and connection you experienced during this exercise.

Chapter 5: Nurturing Faith and Patience

Building patience and faith during periods of waiting is not merely about biding time until God's plans unfold. It involves actively engaging in practices that cultivate a deeper trust in His timing and a stronger reliance on His promises. This part of the journey requires a commitment to growth and the understanding that every moment of waiting is an opportunity for spiritual deepening.

Exercise 10: Patience-Building Scripture Reflection involves selecting passages from the Bible that focus on the virtues of patience and trust in God. For example, James 1:2-4 encourages believers to consider trials as joy because the testing of faith develops perseverance. Reflecting on such scriptures daily can transform our perspective on waiting, teaching us to view each moment of delay as a step closer to spiritual maturity.

Exercise 11: Faith-Strengthening Prayer Routine is about establishing a daily time dedicated to prayer, where the focus is on seeking God's strength to remain steadfast in faith. This exercise encourages the articulation of personal fears and anxieties related to waiting and the surrender of these feelings to God. Through consistent prayer, individuals can experience a shift from anxiety to anticipation, trusting that God is working even in the silence.

Exercise 12: Waiting with Grace Meditation involves practicing mindfulness and presence in the current moment, acknowledging feelings of impatience or frustration without judgment, and then releasing them. This can be done through guided Christian meditation that focuses on the peace and assurance found in God's presence. By meditating on God's character and His promises, individuals can find a serene acceptance of His timeline, replacing restlessness with peace.

Incorporating these exercises into daily life not only assists in developing patience and faith but also shifts the focus from the outcome to the growth experienced in the process of waiting. It's about recognizing that God is shaping us for what is to come and that His timing is always perfect. Through reflective scripture reading, dedicated prayer, and meditative practices, we learn to wait with grace, fully confident in the faithfulness of God to fulfill His promises.

The Virtue of Patience in Scripture

Patience, as depicted throughout Scripture, is not merely a passive waiting but an active engagement in faith. The Bible is rich with examples of individuals who exhibited extraordinary patience as they awaited God's promises to unfold. Abraham's journey, for instance, exemplifies patience in God's timing. Despite the human impossibility of Sarah's pregnancy, Abraham waited decades for the fulfillment of God's promise of a son. This narrative teaches us the significance of trusting in God's timing, even when it contradicts human logic or desires.

Similarly, the story of Joseph, sold into slavery by his brothers, later rising to prominence in Egypt, underscores the essence of patience intertwined with divine purpose. Joseph's patience during years of suffering and imprisonment was rewarded when he was elevated to a position where he could save nations from famine. His story is a testament to the belief that God's plans are always at work, even in the midst of our trials and waiting periods.

Exercise 10: Patience-Building Scripture Reflection and **Exercise 11: Faith-Strengthening Prayer Routine**, previously discussed, are complemented by the practice of identifying with biblical characters. Reflecting on their stories can inspire believers today to cultivate patience and trust in God's plan for their lives. By studying these narratives, individuals can gain insight into the purposeful waiting and see their own waiting periods as opportunities for growth and deepening of faith.

Exercise 12: Waiting with Grace Meditation further enhances this understanding by encouraging a meditative focus on the peace and assurance found in God's presence. This practice allows for a serene acceptance of God's timeline, fostering a peace that surpasses the immediate desire for resolution.

The virtue of patience, therefore, is not a passive resignation but an active, faith-filled waiting on God. It involves a steadfast trust in His promises, a commitment to remain faithful during periods of uncertainty, and a calm assurance that God is working for our good in all things. By embracing the biblical model of patience, believers can navigate the challenges of life with a peace that comes from knowing they are in God's hands.

Waiting on God's Timing with Grace

In the midst of life's uncertainties and the periods of waiting that test our faith, it is essential to remember that grace is not just a concept to be understood but a practice to be lived. Grace in waiting involves a deliberate shift from impatience to a state of spiritual rest, acknowledging that our timelines are not always aligned with the divine schedule. This acceptance does not negate the presence of desires or the essence of our prayers but enriches them with a deeper trust in divine wisdom.

Developing a Mindset of Graceful Acceptance

To cultivate this mindset, one can begin by reflecting on the nature of God's promises. The Scriptures are filled with assurances that are not bound by human constraints of time. For instance, the story of Noah and the flood illustrates a period of waiting that was necessary for the fulfillment of God's plan for humanity. By meditating on such examples, we learn to appreciate the value of divine timing over our immediate expectations.

Engaging in Practices That Foster Patience

1. **Scripture Memorization**: Committing verses about patience and trust to memory serves as a constant reminder of God's faithfulness. Verses like Romans 8:25, "But if we hope for what we do not yet have, we wait for it patiently," can be a source of strength during times of uncertainty.

2. **Gratitude Journaling**: Keeping a record of past prayers answered and blessings received shifts the focus from what is lacking to what has been generously given. This practice fosters an attitude of thankfulness, which is a cornerstone of graceful waiting.

3. **Community Sharing**: Engaging in conversations with fellow believers about the times they had to wait on God's timing can offer perspective and encouragement. These testimonies of faith and patience can be a source of inspiration and a reminder that one is not alone in their journey.

Embracing the Lessons in the Waiting

Waiting is more than a passage of time; it is an opportunity for growth and deepening of faith. During these periods, individuals are called to engage more profoundly with their spiritual practices, to seek understanding and wisdom in Scripture, and to strengthen their relationship with God through prayer. It is a time for self-reflection, for identifying the areas of life where one needs to relinquish control and trust in the divine plan.

Practicing Mindfulness and Presence

Mindfulness practices can be adapted to enhance spiritual patience, encouraging a focus on the present moment and finding peace in the now, rather than being consumed by future outcomes. This can involve silent prayer, meditative reading of Scripture, or simply sitting in silence, acknowledging God's presence in the current moment.

Fostering Spiritual Resilience

The ability to wait with grace is also an exercise in building spiritual resilience. This resilience enables believers to withstand the challenges that come with delays and to emerge from these periods strengthened in their faith and more aligned with God's purposes. It is about finding joy and peace in the promise of what is to come, while also cherishing the journey that leads there.

By integrating these practices into daily life, believers can transform the experience of waiting from a test of patience into an opportunity for spiritual enrichment. It becomes a period marked not by passivity but by active engagement in the process of becoming more attuned to the divine will, ready to receive God's blessings with open hearts and minds, whenever they may come.

3 Exercises for Patience and Faith

Exercise 10: Patience-Building Scripture Reflection

Objective: To cultivate patience and reinforce faith through reflective engagement with Scripture, focusing on passages that emphasize waiting on God's timing and trusting in His plans.

Step-by-step instructions:

1. **Select a Scripture Passage:** Begin by choosing a scripture that speaks to the theme of patience or waiting on God. Examples include Isaiah 40:31, Psalm 27:14, or James 5:7-8. Write down the passage you select.

2. **Create a Reflective Atmosphere:** Find a quiet, comfortable place where you can sit undisturbed for a while. You may choose to light a candle or play soft instrumental music to help set a contemplative mood.

3. **Read the Scripture Aloud:** Read your chosen passage aloud slowly, allowing the words to resonate. Listen to the sound of your own voice as you articulate each word, paying attention to any phrases that strike a chord within you.

4. **Meditate on the Passage:** Close your eyes and meditate on the scripture you just read. Think about what it means to wait on God and the promise of strength for those who do. Consider how this applies to your current life situations where patience is required.

5. **Personalize the Scripture:** Reopen your eyes and rewrite the scripture in your own words, making it personal to your life. For instance, if the scripture is Isaiah 40:31, you might write, "I will gain new strength as I wait on the Lord; He will lift me up on wings like eagles."

6. **Identify Areas Requiring Patience:** Reflect on areas of your life where you find it challenging to be patient. Write these down, acknowledging your feelings and the difficulty in waiting.

7. **Pray for Patience:** Bring your reflections and the areas of impatience before God in prayer. Ask for His strength to endure and for the faith to trust in His timing. Use the

scripture you've personalized as part of your prayer, affirming your trust in God's promises.

8. **Journal Your Insights:** After prayer, journal about your experience with this exercise. Note any insights you gained about patience and how the scripture spoke to you. Write about how you can apply this patience in your daily life.

9. **Commit to Daily Reminders:** Choose one phrase from the scripture you meditated on that particularly speaks to you. Write it down on a small card or note and place it somewhere you will see it daily, like your bathroom mirror or car dashboard, as a reminder to practice patience.

10. **Share Your Experience:** Consider sharing your insights and the scripture that you worked with a friend, family member, or small group. Discussing your journey can provide additional perspectives and encouragement to continue growing in patience and faith.

11. **Repeat Regularly:** Make this exercise a regular part of your spiritual routine, selecting new passages to meditate on and apply to your life. Over time, this practice will help deepen your patience, faith, and trust in God's timing.

Exercise 11: Faith-Strengthening Prayer Routine

Objective: To develop a prayer routine that strengthens faith through consistent, focused communication with God, integrating scripture and personal reflection to deepen trust and patience in God's timing.

Step-by-step instructions:

1. **Select a Time and Place:** Choose a consistent time and quiet place for your daily prayer, where you won't be interrupted. Early morning or late evening are often times of natural stillness that can help in focusing your mind and heart on God.

2. **Gather Your Materials:** Have your Bible, a notebook, and a pen ready. These tools will assist you in recording insights, prayers, and scripture that speak to you during this time.

3. **Begin with Gratitude:** Start your prayer routine by thanking God for His blessings and presence in your life. Acknowledging God's goodness sets a foundation of trust and opens your heart to His guidance.

4. **Read a Scripture Passage:** Choose a passage that focuses on faith, patience, or trust in God. Read it slowly, allowing the words to resonate with you. Consider using a Bible reading plan focused on these themes for structure.

5. **Reflect on the Scripture:** Meditate on the passage, asking yourself what it reveals about God's character and His promises. Write down any thoughts or questions that arise, pondering how the scripture applies to your life.

6. **Pray for Faith and Patience:** Using the insights from your scripture reading, pray specifically for an increase in faith and patience. Ask God to help you trust in His timing and plan for your life, especially in areas where you are seeking answers or direction.

7. **Offer Your Concerns to God:** Share your worries, fears, and desires with God, speaking openly about what's on your heart. Use this time to surrender your concerns to Him, trusting in His care and provision.

8. **Listen for God's Guidance:** After sharing, spend a few moments in silence, listening for God's response. This might come as a sense of peace, a prompting in your heart, or even clarity on a situation you've been praying about.

9. **Write Down Insights and Commitments:** Journal any insights you gain or commitments you feel led to make during your prayer time. Writing these down can help solidify them in your mind and serve as reminders of God's guidance and your intentions.

10. **Close with Praise:** End your prayer time by praising God for who He is and expressing your trust in Him. Singing a hymn, reading a psalm aloud, or simply speaking words of adoration can be powerful ways to conclude.

11. **Review Your Prayer Journal Weekly:** Once a week, take time to review your journal entries. Reflect on how God is answering your prayers and where you are seeing growth in your faith and patience. This can be a source of encouragement and a way to see God's active presence in your life.

12. **Adjust as Needed:** As you practice this routine, be open to the Holy Spirit's leading. You may find certain times, scriptures, or practices particularly meaningful. Be flexible and adjust your routine as you grow in your relationship with God.

Exercise 12: Waiting with Grace Meditation

Objective: This exercise aims to cultivate patience and strengthen faith by meditating on the grace of waiting, recognizing that God's timing is perfect and understanding our role in His divine plan.

Step-by-step instructions:

1. **Select a Scripture Focused on Waiting:** Begin by choosing a Bible verse that speaks to the theme of waiting or God's timing. Psalms 27:14, "Wait for the Lord; be strong, and let your heart take courage; wait for the Lord!" is an excellent place to start.

2. **Find a Peaceful Setting:** Choose a quiet and comfortable spot where you can sit undisturbed. This could be a favorite chair by a window, a spot in your garden, or a secluded area in a local park.

3. **Prepare Your Heart and Mind:** Take several deep breaths to relax your body and mind. With each exhale, release any immediate concerns or distractions. Pray for openness and receptivity to God's word and guidance.

4. **Read the Scripture Aloud:** Slowly read your selected scripture aloud several times. With each reading, allow the words to sink deeper into your spirit, paying attention to any phrases or words that stand out to you.

5. **Reflect on the Meaning of Waiting:** Consider what it means to wait on the Lord. Reflect on the difference between passive waiting and active waiting, where you seek to grow in faith and understanding during the period of waiting.

6. **Meditate on God's Timing:** Contemplate the concept of divine timing. Acknowledge any areas of your life where you are impatiently waiting for change or answers. Offer these situations up to God, affirming your trust in His perfect timing.

7. **Visualize Receiving God's Promises:** With your eyes closed, imagine a future moment where God's promises or guidance become clear to you. Feel the peace and gratitude of that moment, trusting that God will reveal His plan in His time.

8. **Write a Letter to God:** On a piece of paper or in your journal, write a letter to God expressing your thoughts and feelings about waiting. Include your struggles with patience, your desires, and a commitment to trust in His timing.

9. **Pray for Patience and Faith:** Conclude your meditation with a prayer, asking God to fill you with the grace to wait patiently and faithfully. Seek His strength to endure the waiting period with a heart full of trust and peace.

10. **Set a Daily Reminder:** Choose a small object or note as a daily reminder to practice patience and trust in God's timing. Whenever you see it, pause to pray briefly, reaffirming your commitment to wait with grace.

11. **Review Your Letter:** After some time has passed, revisit the letter you wrote to God. Reflect on any changes in your situation or perspective, acknowledging God's hand at work in your life, even in ways you might not have expected.

12. **Share Your Experience:** Consider sharing your experience of waiting with grace with a trusted friend or family member. Discuss how this exercise has impacted your faith and patience, encouraging each other to continue trusting in God's timing.

Chapter 6: The Joy of Gratitude

Gratitude, a transformative emotion, significantly influences our perspective, especially when navigating through life's challenges. By actively practicing thankfulness, we shift our focus from what is lacking to the abundance present in our lives. This change in viewpoint is not just beneficial but essential for maintaining a serene and contented heart. A heart filled with gratitude is less susceptible to the anxieties and stresses that often seek to overwhelm us. **Gratitude Journaling for Perspective Shift** is a powerful tool in this transformative process. This exercise involves dedicating a few moments each day to write down the things for which we are thankful. The act of writing reinforces our feelings of gratitude, making them more tangible and real. It allows us to see, in black and white, the blessings that permeate our lives, often unnoticed during the hustle and bustle of daily living.

Daily Thankfulness Reflection encourages us to end each day by reflecting on moments or things for which we are grateful. This practice helps in embedding a sense of appreciation deep within our psyche, making it a habitual perspective rather than a forced attitude. It's about finding joy in the simple things—a warm cup of coffee, the smile of a loved one, or the serene quiet of the morning before the world wakes up. Recognizing these daily blessings cultivates a profound sense of peace and contentment, which acts as a buffer against the disquiet of life.

Gratitude Letter Writing takes thankfulness a step further by encouraging us to express our gratitude towards others. This exercise not only spreads joy but also strengthens our relationships, creating a supportive community around us. It's a reminder that we are not alone in our journey and that kindness and love surround us, even in unexpected forms. Writing a letter to someone who has made a difference in our lives, no matter how small, reinforces our appreciation for the interconnectedness of human relationships and the impact they have on our well-being.

Gratitude-Focused Prayer integrates our faith into the practice of gratitude, acknowledging God's hand in every gift we receive. This form of prayer is not about asking for more but thanking for what is already present. It's a recognition of God's continuous blessings and an affirmation of our trust in His provision. This spiritual practice deepens our relationship with the divine, grounding our hearts in a state of continuous thankfulness, regardless of our circumstances.

Gratitude Visualization Practice encourages us to create a mental image of the things we are thankful for, enhancing our emotional and psychological connection to them. This practice not only deepens our gratitude but also serves as a calming exercise, reducing stress and increasing feelings of happiness and satisfaction. Visualization helps in solidifying the emotion of gratitude, making it a more prominent part of our emotional landscape.

These exercises serve as foundational practices in cultivating a grateful heart, which is crucial for experiencing true peace and contentment. By embedding these practices into our daily routine, we not only enhance our emotional well-being but also our spiritual health, creating a life that is rich in joy and serenity. This shift in perspective, from a focus on lack to an appreciation for abundance, is a key element in our journey towards lasting peace and fulfillment.

The transformative power of gratitude extends beyond personal well-being, influencing our interactions and the atmosphere around us. By fostering an attitude of thankfulness, we contribute to a culture of positivity and grace, impacting not just our lives but those of people we come into contact with. This ripple effect can transform environments, from homes and workplaces to communities at large, into spaces where kindness and appreciation flourish.

Community Peacebuilding Dialogue embodies this concept by bringing individuals together to share expressions of gratitude, fostering mutual respect and understanding. This dialogue creates a platform for acknowledging the contributions of others, reinforcing the bonds within communities. It serves as a reminder that gratitude is not just an individual practice but a communal one, capable of healing and uniting people.

Collaborative Service Project offers a practical outlet for gratitude, channeling thankfulness into action. By participating in projects that benefit others, individuals can give back to their communities, turning feelings of appreciation into tangible support. This practice not only enriches the lives of recipients but also deepens the sense of gratitude in those who serve, creating a cycle of generosity and thankfulness.

Empathy-Building Group Activity focuses on understanding and appreciating the perspectives and experiences of others. Through activities designed to foster empathy, participants can develop a deeper appreciation for the diversity and richness of human life. This understanding nurtures a grateful heart, aware of the myriad ways in which people enrich our lives and the world around us.

Conflict Resolution Role-Play integrates gratitude into the process of resolving disagreements, highlighting the importance of acknowledging and appreciating the viewpoints of all parties involved. By approaching conflicts with a mindset of gratitude for the opportunity to learn and grow together, individuals can navigate challenges more constructively, leading to resolutions that strengthen relationships rather than strain them.

Incorporating these practices into our lives encourages a shift from a self-centered focus to a more outward-looking perspective, where gratitude becomes a bridge connecting us to others. It's about recognizing that every interaction, every relationship, offers an opportunity to practice gratitude, whether through a simple "thank you," an act of service, or a moment of empathetic listening.

As we weave gratitude into the fabric of our daily lives, we find that it not only transforms our perspective but also our reality. The practice of thankfulness, grounded in faith and expressed through action, becomes a powerful force for change, fostering an environment where peace and contentment can thrive. Through gratitude, we discover the true essence of serenity, a state of being that reflects the depth of our appreciation for life's blessings and the strength of our faith in the goodness that surrounds us.

Counting Our Blessings

In the practice of **gratitude journaling for perspective shift**, individuals are encouraged to set aside a few moments each day to jot down the blessings in their lives. This act of writing not only solidifies our feelings of thankfulness but also serves as a tangible reminder of the abundance that surrounds us. By focusing on what we have rather than what we lack, we cultivate a mindset that appreciates the present moment and fosters a sense of contentment. This exercise is particularly beneficial in moments of stress or anxiety, providing a quick refocusing tool that brings our attention back to the positives in our lives.

Daily thankfulness reflection is another powerful practice that complements gratitude journaling. By ending each day with a reflection on what we are grateful for, we embed a sense of appreciation deep within our psyche. This routine helps in transforming gratitude from a sporadic feeling to a constant state of being. It encourages us to look for the good in each day, even when faced with challenges, and to recognize the small joys and victories that often go unnoticed. This nightly ritual can significantly impact our overall well-being, enhancing our mood and outlook on life.

Gratitude letter writing extends the practice of thankfulness beyond our personal sphere, involving others in our journey of gratitude. This exercise not only amplifies our feelings of appreciation but also strengthens our connections with those around us. By expressing our gratitude towards others, we acknowledge their impact on our lives, fostering a deeper bond and a sense of community. This act of reaching out and sharing our heartfelt thanks can be incredibly rewarding, both for the giver and the receiver, creating a cycle of positivity and mutual appreciation.

Gratitude-focused prayer integrates our spiritual beliefs with the practice of gratitude, offering thanks to God for the blessings in our lives. This form of prayer shifts the focus from petitioning for our needs to acknowledging the abundance already present. It is a powerful way to deepen our faith and trust in God's provision, reinforcing our belief in His goodness and care for us. By regularly engaging in gratitude-focused prayer, we cultivate a more intimate relationship with the divine, grounded in a state of continuous thankfulness.

Gratitude visualization practice involves creating a vivid mental image of the things we are thankful for, enhancing our emotional connection to them. This technique not only deepens our sense of gratitude but also serves as a calming exercise, helping to alleviate stress and promote feelings of happiness and satisfaction. Visualization makes gratitude more palpable, allowing us to fully immerse ourselves in the emotion and its positive effects.

These practices serve as key components in the development of a grateful heart, which is essential for experiencing peace and contentment. By incorporating these exercises into our daily routines, we not only improve our emotional and spiritual health but also create a life characterized by joy and serenity. This shift in perspective, from focusing on what we lack to appreciating the abundance around us, is a crucial step in our journey towards lasting peace and fulfillment.

Gratitude-focused prayer and **gratitude visualization practice** remind us of the importance of looking beyond our immediate circumstances and recognizing the broader spectrum of blessings that life offers. This approach not only enriches our spiritual journey but also enhances our resilience against life's inevitable challenges. By maintaining a grateful heart, we are better equipped to navigate through difficult times with grace and to emerge from them with a strengthened faith and a deeper appreciation for the journey.

Engaging in these gratitude practices encourages a transformative shift in how we perceive and interact with the world around us. It moves us from a state of constant wanting to a state of appreciative receiving. This shift is not merely about changing our thoughts but about transforming our entire approach to life. It fosters a profound sense of well-being that permeates all aspects of our existence, from our relationships to our spiritual practices, enhancing our ability to find peace and contentment in the midst of life's storms.

Incorporating gratitude into our daily routines can also have a profound impact on our physical health. Studies have shown that individuals who regularly practice gratitude report fewer health problems and experience less depression and stress. This is likely due to the positive emotions associated with gratitude, which can improve heart health, boost the immune system, and decrease blood pressure. By adopting gratitude practices, we not only nurture our spiritual and emotional well-being but also contribute to our physical health, creating a holistic approach to living a balanced and serene life.

Moreover, gratitude can play a crucial role in overcoming the barriers to inner peace, such as persistent doubts and fears. By focusing on the blessings we have, we are reminded of the abundance God provides, which can help dispel feelings of scarcity and insecurity. This perspective shift is vital in building a foundation of trust and confidence in God's provision, allowing us to release our anxieties and embrace a life of peace and contentment.

As we cultivate a lifestyle of gratitude, we also become conduits of peace and joy to those around us. Our transformed outlook can inspire others to adopt a similar stance, creating a ripple effect that promotes a culture of appreciation and contentment. This communal aspect of gratitude underscores the interconnectedness of our spiritual journeys, highlighting the importance of supporting one another in our quest for serenity.

Gratitude visualization practice, in particular, serves as a powerful tool for reinforcing these concepts. By vividly imagining the blessings in our lives, we not only deepen our appreciation for them but also solidify our commitment to maintaining a grateful outlook. This practice can be especially helpful in moments of stress or discouragement, providing a quick and effective means of recentering our focus on God's faithfulness and the abundance of His blessings.

In conclusion, the journey towards lasting peace and fulfillment is greatly enhanced by the practice of gratitude. These exercises—**gratitude journaling for perspective shift, daily thankfulness reflection, gratitude letter writing, gratitude-focused prayer**, and **gratitude visualization practice**—are not mere activities but are profound spiritual disciplines that can transform our lives. By integrating these practices into our daily routines, we open our hearts to receive the peace and contentment that God promises, grounding our lives in a deep and abiding sense of gratitude.

Gratitude in Trials

In the midst of hardship, finding joy may seem like a distant, even impossible, goal. However, the practice of gratitude can illuminate the path through the darkest valleys of our lives. When faced with trials, it's natural to focus on the pain, the uncertainty, and the struggle. Yet, it is precisely in these moments that gratitude can become a powerful catalyst for transformation. By shifting our focus from what we lack to the blessings that remain, even in hardship, we open our hearts to the possibility of joy and peace that transcends our circumstances.

Gratitude in the Midst of Trials involves a deliberate and sometimes challenging reorientation of our thoughts and emotions. It requires us to look beyond the immediate discomfort and to find the silver linings that exist even in the darkest clouds. This might mean appreciating the support of loved ones, the comfort of faith, or the growth that comes from enduring adversity. It's about recognizing that, while we may not choose our trials, we can choose our response to them.

The practice of **Finding Joy in Hardship** does not deny the reality of suffering. Rather, it acknowledges the complexity of human experience, where sorrow and joy can coexist. It's about finding moments of beauty, kindness, and strength that emerge in tough times. These moments, no matter how small, are like beacons of hope guiding us towards a deeper understanding of joy and peace.

Cultivating a Heart of Gratitude during difficult times can start with simple, yet profound, steps:

1. **Acknowledge Your Feelings**: Before you can find gratitude in trials, it's important to acknowledge your feelings of pain, loss, or frustration. Accepting these emotions as valid responses to your situation is the first step towards healing.

2. **Seek Out the Good**: Even in the worst of times, there are glimmers of good around us. It might be the kindness of a friend, the beauty of a sunset, or a moment of quiet in a hectic day. Actively looking for these can shift our focus and lift our spirits.

3. **Express Your Gratitude**: Whether through prayer, journaling, or conversation, expressing gratitude helps to solidify the feelings of thankfulness in our hearts. It reinforces our awareness of the good in our lives, even amidst trials.

4. **Practice Mindfulness**: Being present in the moment allows us to appreciate the small blessings that we might otherwise overlook. Mindfulness can help us find joy in the simple aspects of our daily lives, providing a counterbalance to our struggles.

5. **Lean on Your Faith**: For many, faith is a source of comfort and strength in hard times. Turning to scripture, prayer, or spiritual community can provide a deep well of gratitude and hope to draw from.

6. **Share Your Gratitude with Others**: Sharing your journey of finding gratitude in hardship can be both healing for you and inspiring for others. It creates a sense of community and shared resilience that can lighten the load during difficult times.

As we navigate through trials with a heart tuned to gratitude, we begin to see our circumstances in a new light. This shift in perspective doesn't happen overnight, and it's often a process of two steps forward, one step back. However, the effort to find and focus on the blessings in our lives, even when they seem overshadowed by challenges, is a powerful act of faith and resilience. It's a testament to the human spirit's capacity to seek out light in the darkness, to find joy in hardship, and to choose gratitude when it would be easier to succumb to despair.

Gratitude during these trying times not only serves as a personal beacon of light but also as a testament to those around us. It demonstrates the power of a positive outlook and the strength that comes from a steadfast faith. **Engaging in Acts of Service** is another way to cultivate gratitude. By focusing on the needs of others, we often gain a new perspective on our own struggles. Acts of kindness, whether big or small, can provide a sense of purpose and fulfillment that feeds our souls and fosters a grateful heart.

Reflecting on Past Triumphs and Trials can also deepen our sense of gratitude. Remembering how we've navigated past hardships with grace can give us confidence that we will overcome current challenges. This reflection can be a source of motivation, reminding us of our resilience and God's faithfulness through every season of life.

Creating a Gratitude Ritual can anchor us during tumultuous times. This could be as simple as saying three things you're thankful for each night before bed or lighting a candle each morning to reflect on the blessings of a new day. Rituals provide structure and a sense of normalcy that can be comforting in times of chaos.

The Power of Music and Worship should not be underestimated in cultivating a grateful heart. Songs of praise and worship can uplift our spirits and remind us of God's love and promises. Music has the unique ability to bypass our troubled minds and speak directly to our hearts, encouraging a state of gratitude and worship even in the midst of trials.

Connecting with Nature offers a unique perspective on gratitude. The beauty and complexity of the natural world can be a powerful reminder of God's creativity and care. Time spent in nature can be a peaceful respite from the stresses of life, prompting reflections on the blessings of creation and our place within it.

Embracing Community Support plays a crucial role in finding joy in hardship. Being part of a faith community provides not only emotional support but also practical help during difficult times. Sharing our burdens and victories with others can multiply our joys and divide our sorrows, making the journey through trials a shared, and therefore more bearable, experience.

As we incorporate these practices into our lives, we begin to notice a shift in our internal landscape. The storms may rage on around us, but within, we find a sanctuary of peace and gratitude. This inner transformation is not a denial of the pain or difficulty of our circumstances but a choice to focus on the unshakeable truth of God's goodness and love.

Remembering God's Promises is essential in maintaining a grateful heart in the face of adversity. Scriptures that speak of God's faithfulness, provision, and love can be a lifeline in moments of despair. Holding onto these promises allows us to stand firm in our faith, confident that even in our trials, we are never forgotten or forsaken.

Gratitude as a Lifestyle is the ultimate goal. It's about more than just finding silver linings in difficult times; it's about living each day with an awareness of and appreciation for God's gifts. This lifestyle of gratitude doesn't ignore the reality of suffering but chooses to trust in God's plan and presence through it all.

As we practice gratitude consistently, we build a foundation that can withstand life's storms. We learn to see beyond our immediate circumstances to the eternal love and grace that surrounds us. This vision transforms not only our hearts but also our actions, leading us to live out our gratitude in ways that bless those around us and honor God.

Gratitude in the face of trials is a journey of faith, a testament to the belief that joy can be found in all circumstances when our hearts are aligned with God's. It's a choice to celebrate the beauty of life, even when the skies are gray, and to trust in the promise of God's unending faithfulness. Through this practice, we not only survive our trials but thrive, bearing witness to the transformative power of a grateful heart.

5 Exercises for a Grateful Heart

Exercise 1: Gratitude Journaling for Perspective Shift

Objective: To shift perspective through the practice of gratitude journaling, fostering a heart of thankfulness and recognizing God's blessings in daily life, thereby reducing feelings of anxiety and stress.

Step-by-step instructions:

1. **Select a Journal:** Choose a notebook or journal specifically for this exercise. Opt for one that feels special or inspiring to you, as this will be a dedicated space for acknowledging and reflecting on God's gifts in your life.

2. **Set Aside Daily Time:** Dedicate a specific time each day for your gratitude journaling. Early morning or before bedtime are ideal moments for reflection, but choose a time that integrates smoothly into your daily routine.

3. **Begin with Prayer:** Start each journaling session with a short prayer, asking God to open your heart and mind to recognize the blessings He has placed in your life, even in the midst of challenges.

4. **List Three Blessings:** Write down three things you are grateful for each day. These can range from significant life events to simple pleasures or moments of beauty. Try to identify different blessings each day to broaden your awareness of God's constant presence and generosity.

5. **Elaborate on One Blessing:** Select one of the three blessings and write a few sentences about why this particular gift is meaningful to you. Delve into how it impacts your life, what it teaches you about God's character, or how it has helped you grow spiritually or emotionally.

6. **Reflect on Scripture:** Incorporate a Bible verse that relates to gratitude or God's blessings. Write it in your journal and reflect on how this scripture deepens your understanding of the day's blessings. This step connects your gratitude practice with your faith, grounding your thankfulness in God's promises.

7. **Acknowledge Challenges:** Briefly acknowledge any challenges or difficulties you faced during the day. Then, write down at least one way you can see God working through these situations for your good. This encourages a perspective shift, helping you to see God's hand even in hardship.

8. **Pray in Thanksgiving:** Conclude your journaling with a prayer of thanksgiving, offering back to God the gratitude for all the blessings He has poured into your life. This not only seals your gratitude practice for the day but also reinforces your relationship with God through a thankful heart.

9. **Review Weekly:** At the end of each week, take time to review your entries. Reflect on the variety and depth of blessings you've noted and consider any patterns or new insights about God's work in your life. This review can deepen your sense of gratitude and trust in God's provision.

10. **Share Your Gratitude:** Once a month, share a significant blessing from your journal with a friend, family member, or in a small group setting. Discussing your experiences of gratitude can encourage others to recognize God's blessings in their own lives, fostering a community of thankfulness.

Exercise 2: Daily Thankfulness Reflection

Objective: Cultivate a heart of gratitude through daily reflection, recognizing and appreciating God's blessings in your life, thereby shifting your perspective towards joy and serenity.

Step-by-step instructions:

1. **Choose a Dedicated Notebook:** Select a notebook or journal specifically for your Daily Thankfulness Reflections. This will be a tangible record of your gratitude journey.

2. **Set Aside Time Each Day:** Dedicate a specific time each day for reflection, ideally in the morning to set a positive tone for the day or in the evening as a way to reflect on the day's blessings. Aim for about 5-10 minutes of uninterrupted time.

3. **Begin with Prayer:** Start your reflection time with a short prayer, inviting God into this space. Ask for His guidance to open your eyes to the blessings that you may overlook in your daily life.

4. **List Three Specific Things:** Each day, write down three specific things you are thankful for. These can range from significant events (e.g., family, health) to simple joys (e.g., a kind word from a stranger, the beauty of a sunrise). The key is specificity and variety each day.

5. **Reflect on Each Item:** For each item listed, spend a moment reflecting on why you are thankful for it. Try to delve deeper than the surface level, considering how each blessing impacts your life and connects you to God's grace.

6. **Acknowledge Challenges:** If you faced challenges during the day, reflect on any hidden blessings or lessons learned from these situations. This can help shift your perspective from one of frustration or disappointment to one of growth and gratitude.

7. **Close with a Prayer of Thanks:** Conclude your reflection time with a prayer, thanking God for the specific blessings you've identified. This not only reinforces your gratitude but also strengthens your relationship with God by acknowledging His active role in your life.

8. **Review Weekly:** At the end of each week, review your entries to see the abundance of blessings in your life. This weekly reflection can offer a powerful perspective shift, especially during difficult times, reminding you of God's unwavering faithfulness.

9. **Share Your Gratitude:** Periodically, share some of your reflections with family or friends. This act of sharing can not only uplift others but also multiply your sense of gratitude as you vocalize your blessings.

10. **Reflect on Growth:** After a month of daily thankfulness reflection, take some time to reflect on any changes in your mood, attitude, or spiritual life. Many find that a consistent practice of gratitude deepens their faith and enhances their overall sense of peace and contentment.

Exercise 3: Gratitude Letter Writing

Objective: To deepen your sense of gratitude and strengthen your relationship with God by writing a letter expressing thankfulness for His blessings and presence in your life.

Step-by-step instructions:

1. **Select a Quiet Time and Place:** Choose a time and location where you won't be disturbed. This could be early in the morning before your day begins or in the evening as you wind down. The key is to find a peaceful moment where you can focus your thoughts and emotions on gratitude.

2. **Pray for Insight:** Before you begin writing, offer a prayer asking God to open your heart and mind to recognize the blessings in your life, even those that may seem small or insignificant. Ask for the Holy Spirit to guide your words.

3. **Reflect on Your Blessings:** Spend a few moments in silent reflection on the blessings in your life. Consider the various aspects of your life where you've seen God's hand at work, such as family, health, provision, and unexpected joys.

4. **Begin Your Letter:** Address the letter to God, starting with a statement of gratitude. For example, "Dear God, I come before you with a heart full of thanksgiving..."

5. **Detail Your Blessings:** Write about the specific blessings you've identified. Describe why each one is meaningful to you and how it has impacted your life. Be as specific as possible to create a vivid picture of God's faithfulness.

6. **Acknowledge Challenges:** If you feel led, mention any challenges or hardships you've faced, expressing gratitude for God's presence and guidance through these times. This can include lessons learned or strength gained from difficult experiences.

7. **Express Your Love and Trust:** Conclude your letter by reaffirming your love for God and your trust in His continued guidance and provision. You might write, "I trust in Your unfailing love and look forward to seeing Your goodness unfold in my life."

8. **Close in Prayer:** After you've finished your letter, close with a prayer of thanksgiving, reading your letter to God as a prayer. Ask for a heart that remains open to recognizing and appreciating God's blessings every day.

9. **Keep or Share Your Letter:** Decide whether to keep your letter in a personal place where you can revisit it or share it with a trusted friend or family member. Sharing can be a powerful way to testify to God's goodness and encourage others in their faith journey.

10. **Make It a Habit:** Consider making gratitude letter writing a regular practice, such as monthly or annually, to continually cultivate a grateful heart and strengthen your relationship with God over time.

Exercise 4: Gratitude-Focused Prayer

Objective: This exercise is designed to deepen your sense of gratitude through prayer, focusing on recognizing and giving thanks for God's blessings in your daily life, thereby fostering a grateful heart and a more peaceful spirit.

Step-by-step instructions:

1. **Prepare Your Space:** Find a quiet, comfortable place where you can be alone and undisturbed. This could be a cozy corner of your home, a serene spot in your garden, or anywhere you feel a strong sense of peace.

2. **Gather Inspirational Materials:** Bring your Bible, a notebook, and a pen. You may also want to include any devotional books or inspirational writings that resonate with you on the theme of gratitude.

3. **Begin with Silence:** Sit quietly for a few moments, focusing on your breathing to calm your mind and heart. Use this time to consciously enter into God's presence, setting aside the distractions of your day.

4. **Invoke the Holy Spirit:** Invite the Holy Spirit into your time of prayer, asking for help to recognize the many ways God has blessed you. Pray for an open heart that is ready to receive and acknowledge every gift from God, seen and unseen.

5. **Read Scripture on Gratitude:** Open your Bible and read passages that speak of thankfulness and gratitude. Psalms 136, 1 Thessalonians 5:16-18, and Philippians 4:6 are excellent starting points. Reflect on the words and how they apply to your life.

6. **List Your Blessings:** In your notebook, start listing the blessings in your life you are grateful for. Include everything from basic needs being met to unexpected joys and the people who enrich your life. Try to list at least ten items, but don't hesitate to add more as they come to mind.

7. **Pray with Gratitude:** Go through your list, presenting each item to God in prayer. With each blessing, offer a prayer of thanks. Be specific about why you are grateful for each one and how it reflects God's love and care for you.

8. **Reflect on Challenges:** Think about recent challenges or difficulties you've faced. Offer prayers of gratitude for God's presence in those times as well, seeking to find and acknowledge the ways God has been working for your good even in hardship.

9. **Commit to a Gratitude Practice:** Decide on a daily or weekly practice to continue acknowledging your blessings. This could be writing down three things you're grateful for each night, sharing your gratitude with a friend or family member, or incorporating thankfulness into your daily prayers.

10. **Close in Worship:** End your prayer time with a song or hymn of thanksgiving, or simply offer words of praise and adoration to God for His endless gifts and unchanging love. Allow this worship to be a joyful celebration of gratitude.

11. **Reflect and Journal:** After your prayer time, spend a few moments journaling about the experience. Note any new insights or feelings that arose during your prayers of gratitude. Reflect on how this practice of gratitude-focused prayer might impact your daily life and spiritual journey.

Exercise 5: Gratitude Visualization Practice

Objective: To cultivate a heart of gratitude by visualizing God's blessings and goodness in your life, thereby shifting your focus from stress and anxiety to thankfulness and peace.

Step-by-step instructions:

1. **Find a Quiet Space:** Choose a peaceful place where you can sit comfortably without interruptions. This could be a cozy corner of your home, a bench in a garden, or any place that feels serene to you.

2. **Prepare Your Mind and Heart:** Take a few deep breaths to center yourself. With each exhale, release any tension or worries. Pray for openness to experience God's presence and to see your life through the lens of gratitude.

3. **Visualize God's Blessings:** Close your eyes and imagine a golden light representing God's love enveloping you. In this light, start visualizing the blessings in your life. Begin with the immediate and tangible, like a warm home or a recent encounter with a friend, then move to the more significant, such as your health or family.

4. **Incorporate Sensory Details:** As you visualize each blessing, engage all your senses. For example, if you're thankful for your home, imagine the warmth of sunlight through the windows, the comfort of your favorite chair, or the smell of coffee in the morning. Make each image as vivid as possible.

5. **Acknowledge Challenges as Blessings:** Gently shift your focus to challenges you've faced. Visualize them not as obstacles but as opportunities for growth, lessons learned, or ways God has strengthened your faith. See how these experiences have contributed to who you are today.

6. **Give Thanks for Unseen Blessings:** Consider the blessings that are on their way to you, the prayers that are being answered in unseen ways, and the future blessings that God has in store. Trust in His timing and goodness.

7. **Wrap Up with a Prayer of Gratitude:** While still in this state of visualization, offer a prayer of thanks to God for the blessings you've visualized. Acknowledge His provision and ask for a heart that remains grateful in all circumstances.

8. **Journal Your Experience:** Open your eyes and take a moment to journal about what you visualized, especially noting any blessings you hadn't thought of before. Write down how this exercise made you feel and any new insights into God's presence in your life.

9. **Practice Daily:** Commit to performing this visualization practice daily, possibly as part of your morning routine. Over time, notice any shifts in your attitude towards life's challenges and your awareness of everyday blessings.

10. **Share the Practice:** Consider sharing this exercise with a friend or family member who might also benefit from cultivating a more grateful heart. Discussing your experiences can deepen your own practice and encourage others in their journey towards gratitude.

11. **Create a Gratitude Visual Reminder:** Design a small visual reminder of this practice, such as a bookmark with a favorite scripture about gratitude or a photo collage of blessings in your life. Place it somewhere you will see it daily to prompt you to maintain a grateful perspective.

Would you like to listen to this book?

Scan the QrCode below and download the

Audio Version

Chapter 7: Community and Support

In the fabric of our lives, the threads of community and support are interwoven deeply, acting as the scaffold that holds us up during our weakest moments and elevates us during our triumphs. The essence of fellowship, as depicted in scriptures, underscores the importance of walking alongside one another, bearing each other's burdens, and uplifting one another in prayer and encouragement. This chapter delves into the profound role that fellowship plays in the healing process of anxiety, highlighting how shared experiences, empathy, and the collective strength found in faith communities can serve as a powerful antidote to the feelings of isolation that often accompany anxiety.

The act of sharing our journey with others does more than just alleviate loneliness; it mirrors the biblical principle that we are, indeed, our brother's and sister's keeper. Engaging in a faith community provides a unique form of support that transcends mere companionship, offering spiritual nourishment, accountability, and a sense of belonging. These elements are crucial for anyone navigating the turbulent waters of anxiety. When we gather, whether in worship, small groups, or prayer meetings, we are reminded that we are not alone in our struggles. The collective faith of the community acts as a beacon of hope, guiding us back to a place of peace and serenity.

Moreover, the power of testimony within these groups cannot be overstated. Hearing how others have overcome obstacles, including anxiety, through their faith and trust in God serves as a potent reminder of His faithfulness and provision. These stories of victory not only inspire but also embolden us to face our own challenges with renewed strength and confidence. It is in these moments of vulnerability and shared understanding that we often find the most profound connections with others, fostering an environment where healing can truly begin.

Additionally, the role of spiritual leaders and mentors in guiding us through our journey of overcoming anxiety is invaluable. These individuals, who have often navigated their own trials, can offer wisdom, insight, and direction that is both biblically sound and personally empathetic. They serve as living examples of how to steadfastly rely on God's promises, even when the path ahead seems obscured by worry and fear.

As we consider the importance of community and support in our journey toward serenity, it becomes clear that the path to peace is not one that should be walked alone. The collective wisdom, strength, and encouragement of a faith-based community provide a solid foundation upon which we can build a life marked by tranquility and trust in God's unchanging promises. This chapter aims to explore the various ways in which engaging with our spiritual family can fortify our hearts, renew our minds, and transform our experiences with anxiety into opportunities for growth and deeper faith.

Engagement in service projects and outreach initiatives presents another dimension where community and support play a critical role in mitigating anxiety. By focusing outward, individuals can experience a shift in perspective that highlights the interconnectedness of human experiences and the impact of collective action. This outward focus not only diverts attention from personal anxieties but also cultivates a sense of purpose and fulfillment derived from contributing to the well-being of others. Such activities reinforce the concept that, through service, one can find a deeper sense of peace and satisfaction that transcends individual concerns.

The practice of communal worship also holds significant therapeutic value. Coming together to praise and worship creates an atmosphere where individuals can lay down their burdens and find comfort in the presence of God and fellow believers. In these moments, the power of music, prayer, and the spoken word converge to uplift spirits and foster an environment where peace can flourish. The act of worship, both as a personal and communal endeavor, serves to realign our focus towards God, reminding us of His sovereignty and the peace that comes from surrendering our anxieties to Him.

Moreover, engaging in Bible study groups offers a platform for deeper exploration of faith and its application in overcoming anxiety. These settings provide a safe space for open dialogue, questions, and reflections on Scripture that directly addresses the concerns and challenges individuals may face. Through shared insights and collective learning, participants can uncover new strategies for managing anxiety, grounded in biblical truths and supported by the empathy and understanding of peers.

The role of accountability within these community structures cannot be overlooked. Having someone to share goals, struggles, and progress with can significantly enhance an individual's journey towards managing anxiety. Accountability partners or groups encourage consistency in spiritual disciplines, offer constructive feedback, and celebrate milestones together. This mutual support system reinforces the notion that growth and healing are ongoing processes that benefit from shared experiences and collective wisdom.

Finally, the establishment of a supportive faith community acts as a sanctuary for those grappling with anxiety. It is within this community that individuals can find a family bound not by blood but by faith and shared aspirations for serenity and peace. The sense of belonging and acceptance found in such communities validates personal experiences while providing a framework for collective healing and support.

In essence, the fabric of community and support is integral to the journey towards overcoming anxiety and discovering lasting serenity. It is through the combined efforts of individual faith, shared experiences, and collective action that the path to peace becomes illuminated. By embracing the support of our spiritual family, engaging in service, participating in worship and study, and holding each other accountable, we can navigate the challenges of anxiety with strength, hope, and the assurance of God's unchanging promises.

The Role of Fellowship in Healing Anxiety

Building upon the foundation of communal support, it is crucial to delve into the practical aspects of fostering fellowship within our faith communities to address anxiety. One effective approach is the creation of **support groups** specifically designed for those struggling with anxiety. These groups offer a safe space for sharing personal experiences, challenges, and victories. They become a platform for mutual understanding and empathy, where individuals can speak openly about their struggles without fear of judgment. The shared experiences within these groups often lead to deep, meaningful connections that can significantly alleviate feelings of isolation and loneliness that accompany anxiety.

Another vital component of fellowship in healing anxiety is the **mentorship program**. Pairing individuals who have navigated the complexities of anxiety with those currently facing them can be incredibly beneficial. Mentors provide guidance, share coping strategies, and offer spiritual support, drawing from their personal journeys and insights. This one-on-one relationship creates a unique opportunity for personalized support and encouragement, grounded in faith and shared experiences.

Service and volunteer opportunities within the community also play a significant role in combating anxiety. Engaging in acts of service shifts focus from self to others, fostering a sense of purpose and fulfillment. It is through serving that individuals can experience the joy of giving, witness the tangible impact of their actions, and feel connected to a larger purpose. Organizing community outreach programs, charity events, or mission trips encourages participation and strengthens the bonds within the community, creating a supportive network that extends beyond the church walls.

Incorporating **faith-based workshops and seminars** that address mental health and anxiety from a biblical perspective can equip individuals with knowledge and tools to manage their anxiety. These educational sessions can cover topics such as stress management, mindfulness, and the importance of prayer and meditation in achieving peace. By providing a space for learning and discussion, the community can foster an environment of growth and empowerment.

Regular community gatherings, such as potlucks, picnics, or retreats, offer additional opportunities for fellowship. These less formal settings allow individuals to build relationships, share life experiences, and support one another in a relaxed and welcoming environment. It is in these gatherings that the community can come together to celebrate victories, offer comfort in times of struggle, and simply enjoy the company of fellow believers.

Prayer circles constitute a powerful means of support, enabling members to come together to pray for one another's needs, concerns, and anxieties. This collective prayer effort not only uplifts the individuals being prayed for but also strengthens the faith of those praying. Witnessing prayers being answered can reinforce the community's trust in God's provision and timing, fostering a shared sense of hope and encouragement.

In conclusion, the role of fellowship in healing anxiety encompasses a multifaceted approach that includes support groups, mentorship, service opportunities, educational workshops, social gatherings, and prayer circles. Each of these elements contributes to building a supportive, empathetic, and engaged community where individuals struggling with anxiety can find comfort, understanding, and practical assistance. Through these communal efforts, the church can become a beacon of hope, offering a pathway to peace and serenity grounded in faith and fellowship.

Building a Supportive Faith Community

Creating a supportive faith community involves more than just regular gatherings; it requires intentional actions and structures that foster an environment of encouragement, learning, and mutual support. One of the foundational steps in this process is the establishment of **small group ministries**. These groups, often centered around specific life stages, interests, or topics, provide a more intimate setting for members to connect, share personal experiences, and grow together spiritually. By focusing on commonalities, these small groups can address the unique needs of their members, offering tailored support and fostering closer relationships.

Another critical aspect is the **integration of new members** into the community. Welcoming newcomers and integrating them into the life of the church through orientation sessions, welcome committees, or buddy systems helps to ensure that everyone feels valued and included. This not only aids in the retention of members but also strengthens the overall sense of community. Providing clear pathways for involvement allows new members to quickly find their place and contribute to the community, enhancing the collective experience.

Intercessory prayer teams play a vital role in a supportive faith community. These teams dedicate themselves to praying for the needs of the congregation and its members, interceding on behalf of those facing challenges, and thanking God for blessings and answered prayers. The commitment to pray for one another deepens communal bonds and reinforces the belief in the power of prayer to effect change.

Educational programs that offer biblical instruction and life skills training are essential for personal and communal growth. Classes and workshops that cover topics such as biblical studies, marriage enrichment, parenting, financial stewardship, and mental health not only equip individuals with valuable knowledge but also create opportunities for members to interact and learn from one another. These programs can be pivotal in addressing the practical and spiritual needs of the community.

The **celebration of milestones and achievements** within the community is another way to build a supportive environment. Recognizing birthdays, anniversaries, graduations, and other significant events in the lives of members fosters a sense of belonging and shows that the community values each person as an individual. These celebrations can be incorporated into regular services or special events, ensuring that members feel appreciated and connected.

Outreach and mission initiatives provide the community with a shared purpose and vision. By participating in local outreach projects or international missions, members can experience the joy and fulfillment that come from serving others and spreading the message of faith. These activities not only impact the lives of those being served but also strengthen the bonds among those who serve, creating a deeper sense of unity and purpose within the community.

The role of **leadership development** cannot be overstated in building a supportive faith community. Investing in the training and mentoring of future leaders ensures the sustainability and vitality of the community. Leadership programs should focus on developing spiritual maturity, leadership skills, and a heart for service, preparing individuals to take on roles of responsibility within the community and beyond.

Regular social events and gatherings outside of formal worship services offer additional opportunities for connection and fellowship. Picnics, sports events, concerts, and other social activities provide a relaxed atmosphere for members to enjoy each other's company and build friendships. These events are crucial for creating a sense of family among members, where relationships can flourish in a less structured environment.

Technology and social media can also be leveraged to enhance community support. Online prayer groups, virtual Bible studies, and social media platforms offer avenues for connection and engagement, especially for those who are unable to attend in-person events. Utilizing technology ensures that all members, regardless of their physical location or circumstances, can remain an active part of the community.

By implementing these strategies, faith communities can create a supportive environment where members feel valued, connected, and empowered to grow in their faith. Through intentional actions and structures, communities can ensure that every member has the opportunity to contribute to and benefit from the collective journey of faith.

4 Exercises for Community Engagement

Exercise 1: Community Peacebuilding Dialogue

Objective: This exercise aims to foster a deeper sense of community and peace by engaging in meaningful dialogue that bridges differences and builds understanding within a faith-based context.

Step-by-step instructions:

1. **Gather a Diverse Group:** Organize a meeting with individuals from your faith community, ensuring a diverse mix of ages, backgrounds, and perspectives. Aim for a group size of 8-12 participants to allow for a variety of viewpoints while maintaining an intimate setting for meaningful conversation.

2. **Select a Neutral Venue:** Choose a neutral, comfortable space for the dialogue, such as a community center, a quiet park, or a church hall. Ensure the setting is conducive to open, respectful conversation without distractions.

3. **Set Ground Rules:** Begin the session by establishing ground rules to create a safe and respectful environment. Emphasize the importance of active listening, withholding judgment, and allowing each person to speak without interruption.

4. **Choose a Facilitator:** Appoint a facilitator who is skilled in guiding discussions and managing group dynamics. The facilitator should be neutral, encouraging participation from all members and ensuring the conversation remains focused and productive.

5. **Prepare Discussion Prompts:** Prior to the meeting, prepare a list of discussion prompts centered around themes of peace, understanding, and faith. These prompts should be open-ended to encourage personal reflection and sharing. Examples include "What does peace mean to you in the context of our faith?" or "Share a time when you felt a deep sense of community and what contributed to it."

6. **Engage in Dialogue:** Use the prepared prompts to guide the dialogue. Each participant should have an opportunity to respond to each prompt, with the facilitator encouraging deeper exploration of ideas and feelings that arise.

7. **Reflect on Shared Values:** Throughout the discussion, highlight shared values and common ground that emerge. Encourage participants to reflect on how these shared values can be the foundation for building a stronger, more peaceful community.

8. **Encourage Action Steps:** As the dialogue concludes, invite participants to suggest practical action steps that the group can take to promote peace and understanding within the wider community. This could include organizing community service projects, hosting regular dialogue sessions, or creating a shared declaration of commitment to peace.

9. **Close with a Shared Moment of Reflection:** End the session with a moment of silent reflection or a group prayer, focusing on the aspirations for peace and unity discussed during the dialogue.

10. **Follow-Up:** Plan a follow-up session to review the progress on the action steps and to continue building the bonds of understanding and peace within the community. Encourage ongoing communication among participants through social media groups or email chains to maintain the momentum of the dialogue.

Exercise 2: Collaborative Service Project

Objective: To foster a sense of community and shared purpose through organizing and participating in a service project that benefits a local charity or community group, thereby embodying the principles of peace, support, and empathy within the community.

Step-by-step instructions:

1. **Identify a Need:** Research and identify a local charity or community group in need of assistance. Consider areas where your group's efforts can make a significant impact, such as a food bank, homeless shelter, or a community clean-up initiative.

2. **Plan the Project:** Gather a planning committee from your faith or community group to outline the project. Decide on the scope, date, and time for the service project. Ensure that the project is feasible and aligns with the group's abilities and resources.

3. **Assign Roles:** Assign specific roles and responsibilities to volunteers based on their skills and interests. Roles might include project leader, supplies coordinator, volunteer recruiter, and publicity coordinator.

4. **Gather Resources:** Determine the resources and materials needed for the project. Organize a drive within your community to gather donations, or seek sponsorships from local businesses to cover costs.

5. **Promote the Project:** Use social media, community bulletin boards, and word of mouth to promote the project and recruit volunteers. Highlight the purpose of the project and the difference it aims to make in the community.

6. **Host a Pre-Event Meeting:** Before the project day, gather all volunteers for a briefing. Discuss the project's goals, expectations, and safety guidelines. This is also an opportunity to foster a sense of unity and purpose among the participants.

7. **Execute the Project:** On the day of the project, ensure that all volunteers are clear on their roles. Begin with a group prayer or moment of reflection, asking for God's guidance and blessing on your efforts to serve the community.

8. **Document the Project:** Take photos and videos during the project to document the effort and its impact. This will be valuable for sharing the success of the project with your community and encouraging future participation.

9. **Reflect Together:** After completing the project, gather the volunteers for a debriefing session. Share experiences, discuss the project's impact, and reflect on the lessons learned about service, community, and faith.

10. **Thank Participants:** Send thank-you notes or emails to all volunteers and sponsors, acknowledging their contributions and the difference they've made. Include highlights and photos from the project to remind them of the positive impact.

11. **Share the Story:** Write an article or blog post about the project, including its purpose, the volunteers' experiences, and its impact on the community. Share this with your community and on social media to inspire others and spread the message of peace and service.

12. **Plan for the Future:** Consider making the service project an annual event or initiating other projects throughout the year. Use feedback from participants to improve and expand your community service efforts, continuing to foster a spirit of compassion and support within your community.

Exercise 3: Empathy-Building Group Activity

Objective: To foster empathy and understanding within a faith community by engaging in an activity designed to share and understand each other's life experiences and challenges, thereby building a stronger, more supportive community.

Step-by-step instructions:

1. **Organize a Group Meeting:** Schedule a gathering with your faith community, small group, or bible study group. Ensure the setting is comfortable and conducive to open, heartfelt communication.

2. **Set the Tone:** Begin the meeting with a prayer, inviting God's presence and asking for open hearts and minds. Emphasize the importance of confidentiality, respect, and non-judgment in this safe space.

3. **Introduction to Empathy:** Briefly discuss what empathy means—understanding and sharing the feelings of another—and why it is crucial for community support and spiritual growth.

4. **Activity Preparation:** Provide each participant with paper and a pen. Ask them to reflect on a recent challenge or struggle they feel comfortable sharing with the group. Encourage honesty but also respect for personal boundaries.

5. **Sharing in Pairs:** Divide the group into pairs. If the group is large, consider forming small clusters of no more than four individuals. Instruct them to take turns sharing their written reflections, emphasizing the importance of listening without interrupting.

6. **Reflective Listening:** After one person shares, their partner should spend a few minutes reflecting back what they heard, focusing on the emotions and experiences shared. This practice helps deepen understanding and empathy.

7. **Group Sharing (Optional):** Depending on the group's comfort level, invite volunteers to share their experiences and reflections with the entire group. This step can be powerful but should be approached with sensitivity to individual comfort levels.

8. **Discuss the Role of Faith:** Encourage the group to discuss how faith and God's promises can be a source of strength and comfort in the challenges shared. This can include sharing relevant scripture passages or personal testimonies of faith in difficult times.

9. **Prayer Time:** Conclude the activity with a time of prayer, either in the same pairs/small groups or as a whole group. Focus the prayers on asking for God's guidance, strength, and peace for the challenges shared.

10. **Commit to Action:** Challenge each participant to take one action step in the following week to show empathy to someone in their life, whether within the group or

outside it. This could be a follow-up conversation, an offer of help, or a simple act of kindness.

11. **Follow-Up:** Plan a follow-up meeting or check-in to share experiences and reflections on the activity. Discuss any insights gained or how the exercise impacted the group's sense of community and empathy.

Exercise 4: Conflict Resolution Role-Play

Objective: This exercise aims to enhance understanding and practice of conflict resolution within a community setting, fostering an environment of peace and mutual respect grounded in faith principles. Participants will engage in role-play scenarios to develop empathy, listening skills, and effective communication strategies for resolving disagreements in a manner that reflects God's teachings on love, forgiveness, and reconciliation.

Step-by-step instructions:

1. **Form Small Groups:** Divide participants into small groups of 3-4 individuals to create a safe and intimate setting for the role-play exercise.

2. **Select Conflict Scenarios:** Each group is given a set of pre-prepared conflict scenarios that are common within communities, such as disagreements over church activities, misunderstandings between community members, or differing opinions on a community project.

3. **Assign Roles:** Within each group, members randomly select roles from the scenario, ensuring that each person gets the opportunity to play both the role of the person raising a concern and the person responding to the concern.

4. **Prepare:** Allow a few minutes for participants to review their scenarios and roles, encouraging them to think about the emotions, motivations, and perspectives of the characters they are portraying.

5. **Role-Play Begins:** Groups begin the role-play exercise, acting out the conflict scenario while the rest of the group observes. Encourage participants to stay in character, expressing thoughts and feelings as authentically as possible.

6. **Apply Conflict Resolution Techniques:** Encourage the use of conflict resolution techniques such as active listening, expressing feelings without blame, using "I" statements, and seeking common ground. Remind participants to incorporate faith-based principles like forgiveness, patience, and love in their approach.

7. **Group Discussion:** After the role-play, the group discusses the scenario. This should include what was learned about the conflict, the effectiveness of the communication strategies used, and how faith principles can guide conflict resolution.

8. **Reflect on Personal Experiences:** Participants reflect on their own experiences with conflict in their community or personal life. Encourage them to share how they might apply the strategies practiced in the role-play to these real-life situations.

9. **Prayer for Peace:** Conclude the exercise with a group prayer, asking for God's guidance in resolving conflicts and for the grace to approach disagreements with empathy, love, and a willingness to understand others.

10. **Commitment to Action:** Each participant commits to applying at least one conflict resolution strategy or faith principle learned during the exercise in their interactions within the community over the following weeks.

11. **Follow-Up:** Plan a follow-up session where participants can share their experiences of applying what they learned in real-life conflicts, discussing challenges faced and successes achieved.

Chapter 8: Integrating Faith into Daily Life

Integrating faith into daily life is essential for achieving a harmonious balance between the spiritual and the secular. This balance is not always easy to maintain, especially in a world that often seems to operate on principles counter to those we hold dear in our faith. Yet, it is precisely this integration that can transform our daily routines into acts of worship, infusing every moment with divine purpose and significance. The key lies in recognizing that faith is not just for Sundays or special occasions but is a lens through which we can view and experience every aspect of our lives.

Daily Faith Reflection offers a practical starting point for weaving faith into the fabric of our daily existence. By setting aside time each morning to reflect on a passage of Scripture or a devotional thought, we can frame our day within the context of God's promises and guidance. This practice not only strengthens our spiritual foundations but also prepares us to face the day's challenges with grace and wisdom. It's about making an intentional choice to see God's hand at work in our lives, from the mundane to the momentous.

Scripture-Based Goal Setting is another powerful tool for integrating faith into daily life. By aligning our personal and professional goals with biblical principles, we ensure that our pursuits are not only fulfilling but also pleasing to God. This might involve setting goals that foster kindness, generosity, and integrity, or that contribute to our growth as stewards of the talents and resources entrusted to us by our Creator. Such an approach not only sanctifies our ambitions but also provides a clear moral compass guiding our decisions and actions.

Faith-Driven Decision Making involves consulting our faith values and principles before making significant life choices. Whether it's a career move, a financial decision, or a relationship matter, incorporating prayer and scriptural wisdom into the decision-making process can lead to choices that reflect our deepest convictions. This practice encourages a reliance on divine guidance and a trust in God's providence, reminding us that we are not alone in navigating the complexities of life.

Morning Faith Ritual can be as simple as a prayer of gratitude upon waking, a brief meditation on a verse of Scripture, or listening to worship music as we prepare for the day. Establishing such a ritual ensures that our first thoughts and actions are centered on God, setting a positive tone for the day ahead. This ritual acts as a spiritual anchor, keeping us grounded in our faith amidst the flurry of daily responsibilities.

Evening Gratitude Prayer is a reflective practice that helps us recognize and appreciate God's presence and blessings throughout the day. By taking stock of the moments for which we are grateful, we can end our day on a note of thanksgiving, acknowledging God's faithfulness in both the trials and triumphs. This practice not only cultivates a heart of gratitude but also reinforces our awareness of God's active involvement in our lives.

By integrating these practices into our daily routines, we create a life that is not only balanced but also deeply enriched by our faith. Each moment becomes an opportunity to live out our beliefs, to grow in our relationship with God, and to witness to the transformative power of faith in action. As we continue to explore the ways in which we can seamlessly integrate faith into every aspect of our lives, we discover that balance is not just about managing time or priorities but about aligning our entire being with the will and purpose of God.

To further embody faith in our everyday lives, **Community Engagement** emerges as a pivotal aspect. Actively participating in church and community events not only strengthens our connection with fellow believers but also allows us to put our faith into practice. Volunteering for outreach programs, joining Bible study groups, or simply being part of church social events can enrich our spiritual journey and provide avenues for serving others. These activities encourage us to live out the teachings of Christ in tangible ways, fostering a sense of belonging and mutual support that is vital for spiritual growth.

Scripture-Based Goal Setting extends into the realm of personal development and service, guiding us to set objectives that not only benefit ourselves but also contribute positively to the lives of others. Whether it's through acts of charity, mentoring, or participating in community improvement projects, our goals can reflect a commitment to living out our faith in ways that touch the lives of those around us. This intentional approach to goal setting helps ensure that our actions align with our values, creating a ripple effect of positive change within our communities.

Faith-Driven Decision Making becomes particularly relevant when faced with ethical dilemmas or opportunities to stand up for what we believe in. In such instances, our faith provides a moral framework that helps us navigate these challenges with integrity. Whether it's in the workplace, within our families, or among friends, making choices that reflect our faith values can sometimes require courage and conviction. However, it is through these decisions that our faith becomes visible to others, serving as a testament to the transformative power of living a life grounded in spiritual principles.

The **Morning Faith Ritual** and **Evening Gratitude Prayer** serve as bookends to our day, framing each moment with mindfulness of God's presence. But beyond these personal practices, sharing these rituals with family or roommates can amplify their impact. Incorporating faith discussions at meal times, sharing daily devotions, or praying together strengthens familial bonds and fosters a shared spiritual journey. These shared experiences not only enrich our personal faith but also create a nurturing environment for spiritual growth among loved ones.

By adopting these practices, we weave faith into the very fabric of our daily existence, making every action an expression of our spiritual beliefs. This holistic approach to living our faith not only deepens our relationship with God but also influences those around us in meaningful ways. As we strive to balance the demands of daily life with our spiritual commitments, let us remember that each moment offers an opportunity to demonstrate our faith through our actions, decisions, and interactions with others. Through consistent practice and engagement, we can achieve a harmonious balance that reflects the depth of our faith and the sincerity of our commitment to living it out each day.

Keeping Faith at the Center

Fostering a **spiritual journal** can be an invaluable tool for maintaining a focus on faith amidst the hustle and bustle of daily life. This personal record serves not only as a repository for thoughts, prayers, and reflections but also as a physical testament to one's spiritual journey. By dedicating a few minutes each day to jot down insights gained from Scripture, personal revelations, or simply articulating thoughts to God, individuals can cultivate a deeper, more intimate relationship with the divine. This practice encourages a habit of mindfulness regarding one's spiritual health and progress, providing a tangible means to witness God's work in one's life over time.

Setting aside dedicated time for family or communal worship each week beyond traditional Sunday services can significantly reinforce faith's role in daily life. This can take the form of a family devotion night, where members gather to read Scripture, share what they've learned, and pray together. Alternatively, hosting a small group meeting with friends or neighbors to discuss a faith-based book or Bible study can offer communal support and encouragement. These gatherings serve as a regular reminder of God's place in our lives and the lives of those around us, fostering a sense of community and shared faith journey.

Volunteering as a form of worship presents another avenue through which faith can be seamlessly integrated into daily routines. By identifying opportunities to serve within one's church or local community, individuals can live out the teachings of Christ through acts of kindness, service, and love. This outward expression of faith not only benefits those on the receiving end but also enriches the volunteer's spiritual life, offering a practical application of biblical principles and reinforcing the connection between faith and daily actions.

Incorporating faith into decision-making processes is crucial for keeping one's spiritual beliefs at the forefront of daily life. Before making significant decisions, individuals can seek guidance through prayer, consult Scripture, and seek wise counsel from spiritually mature friends or mentors. This practice ensures that choices are aligned with God's will and teachings, fostering a life that reflects one's faith values. It also serves as a constant reminder of the sovereignty of God in all aspects of life, from the mundane to the monumental.

Utilizing technology to bolster faith in today's digital age, numerous resources can help keep one's spiritual life vibrant and active. Subscribing to daily devotional emails, listening to Christian podcasts, or using Bible study apps can provide spiritual nourishment and encouragement anytime, anywhere. These tools make it easier to stay connected with one's faith, even during busy days, by offering accessible ways to engage with Scripture, prayer, and teachings on the go.

Embracing acts of gratitude as a daily practice helps to center one's life around faith by acknowledging God's presence and blessings continuously. This can be as simple as verbally expressing thanks for the day's blessings or maintaining a gratitude list in a journal. Recognizing and celebrating God's handiwork in every aspect of life cultivates an attitude of worship and reliance on Him, reinforcing the belief in His goodness and care regardless of circumstances.

Practicing forgiveness and extending grace in interpersonal relationships mirrors the forgiveness and grace that are central to the Christian faith. By choosing to forgive others and show grace in challenging situations, believers embody Christ's teachings and love, making faith a tangible aspect of daily interactions. This not only impacts the individuals involved but also serves as a powerful witness to the transformative power of faith in one's life.

By integrating these practices into everyday routines, individuals can ensure that their faith remains an active, central force in their lives. Each act, whether big or small, becomes an expression of devotion to God, weaving a rich tapestry of worship that extends beyond the walls of the church and into the world. Through consistent engagement with these practices, believers can navigate the complexities of life with a firm foundation of faith, reflecting the love and teachings of Christ in all they do.

Balancing Work, Family, and Spirituality

Achieving a harmonious balance between work, family, and spirituality often feels like an elusive goal, especially in today's fast-paced world. Yet, it is possible to weave these essential aspects of life into a cohesive whole, ensuring that none is neglected at the expense of the others. The key lies in intentional living and prioritizing, guided by one's faith and values. **Time management** plays a crucial role in this process. Allocating specific times for work, family activities, and spiritual practices can help in maintaining a clear boundary between these areas, preventing one from overshadowing the others. It's about making conscious choices to dedicate quality time to each, ensuring that work commitments do not encroach on family time and that both are balanced with periods dedicated to spiritual growth and reflection.

Setting priorities according to one's values is another vital strategy. This involves evaluating what truly matters in one's life and making decisions that reflect these values. For many, spirituality forms the bedrock of their existence, influencing how they approach work and interact with family. By identifying this core value, individuals can make more informed choices that align with their spiritual beliefs, such as opting for a job that offers flexibility for family commitments or engaging in work that feels meaningful and contributes positively to society.

Open communication with family members about one's spiritual beliefs and how they influence daily life can also foster a supportive environment where each person's needs are acknowledged and respected. Discussing how work commitments and spiritual practices fit into the family schedule encourages cooperation and mutual support, making it easier to find a balance that accommodates everyone's needs.

Incorporating spirituality into daily routines can transform mundane tasks into acts of worship and reflection. Whether it's listening to a devotional podcast on the commute, using breaks to read scripture or pray, or simply maintaining a mindset of gratitude and mindfulness throughout the day, these practices can help in keeping one's faith at the forefront, even amidst the demands of work and family life.

Creating rituals and traditions that involve all family members can also strengthen the bond between work, family, and spirituality. This might include setting aside a regular time for family prayer, attending worship services together, or volunteering as a family in faith-based community service. Such activities not only nurture the family's spiritual life but also create cherished memories and a sense of belonging and purpose.

Seeking community support from one's faith community can provide encouragement and practical assistance in balancing these aspects of life. Many faith communities offer resources such as family counseling, spiritual direction, and support groups for working parents. Engaging with these resources can offer fresh perspectives and strategies for managing the complexities of modern life in a way that honors one's spiritual commitments.

Practicing self-care is an often-overlooked aspect of maintaining balance. Recognizing that one cannot pour from an empty cup, it's essential to include spiritual self-care in one's routine. This could involve personal prayer time, meditation, or participating in retreats and workshops that refresh the spirit and provide nourishment for the soul. By caring for one's spiritual well-being, individuals are better equipped to meet the demands of work and family life with patience, grace, and resilience.

In essence, balancing work, family, and spirituality is not about achieving a perfect equilibrium but about making intentional choices that reflect one's values and priorities. It requires flexibility, communication, and a commitment to living one's faith in all aspects of life. By adopting these practices, individuals can navigate the challenges of modern living while staying true to their spiritual convictions and nurturing their relationships at work and home.

Leveraging technology to maintain this balance is another practical approach. With the advent of mobile apps and online platforms, individuals can now access a wealth of spiritual resources at their fingertips. From bible study apps to online prayer groups, technology offers numerous ways to stay connected with one's faith, even during the busiest days. It also allows for greater flexibility in work arrangements, such as telecommuting, which can free up more time for family and spiritual activities. By thoughtfully integrating technology into daily life, one can find more opportunities to cultivate their spiritual life without sacrificing work or family time.

Prioritizing quality over quantity in time spent with family and in spiritual pursuits is crucial. In a culture that often equates busyness with importance, it's vital to remember that the depth of relationships and spiritual experiences cannot be measured in hours alone. Focusing on meaningful interactions and genuinely engaging in spiritual practices can make the time spent in these areas more fulfilling and impactful. This might mean choosing fewer, but more focused, family activities that allow for real connection or selecting specific spiritual disciplines that resonate deeply with one's faith journey.

Adjusting expectations is a necessary step in finding balance. In a perfect world, one might have ample time for every work project, family activity, and spiritual discipline they wish to pursue. However, reality often requires making tough choices and sometimes saying no to good opportunities to prioritize great ones. By setting realistic expectations and giving oneself grace, it's possible to navigate the inevitable ebbs and flows of life without losing sight of what's truly important.

Celebrating small victories along the way can also provide encouragement and motivation. Recognizing moments when the balance feels right or when a new spiritual insight is gained can serve as reminders of progress and the value of one's efforts. These celebrations, whether personal or shared with family and community, can reinforce the commitment to living a balanced life.

Engaging in regular reflection and reassessment of how well one's work, family, and spiritual life are integrated is key to maintaining balance. Life's circumstances and priorities can change, and what worked well at one time may need adjustment later. Setting aside time to reflect on these areas, perhaps during a weekly review or through journaling, can help identify necessary adjustments and reinforce intentions.

By embracing these strategies, individuals can navigate the complexities of balancing work, family, and spirituality with grace and intentionality. It's a dynamic process that requires ongoing attention and adaptation, but the rewards of a life lived in alignment with one's values and faith are immeasurable. Through deliberate actions and a commitment to prioritizing according to one's spiritual convictions, achieving a fulfilling and harmonious balance is within reach.

5 Exercises for a Faith-Filled Life

Exercise 1: Daily Faith Reflection

Objective: To integrate faith into daily life by reflecting on God's presence and guidance, fostering a deeper connection with Him through daily activities and decisions.

Step-by-step instructions:

1. **Choose a Quiet Time:** Select a quiet time early in the morning or before bed for your daily faith reflection. This should be a time when you can be alone, undisturbed, and focused.

2. **Prepare Your Space:** Find a comfortable and serene spot in your home. You may choose to sit by a window with a view of nature or in a designated prayer corner. Consider lighting a candle or having a small cross or Bible nearby to create a sacred atmosphere.

3. **Begin with Prayer:** Open your reflection time with a prayer, inviting God into this moment. Ask for His wisdom to see His hand at work in your life and for the openness to hear His voice.

4. **Read a Daily Scripture:** Select a verse or passage for daily reading. You can follow a Bible reading plan or choose a book of the Bible to read through. Reflect on the passage, considering its application to your life.

5. **Journal Your Reflections:** In a journal, write down your thoughts on the scripture passage. Note any insights, questions, or personal applications you discern. Reflect on how the passage can influence your actions and decisions for the day.

6. **Contemplate God's Presence:** Spend a few moments in silence, contemplating God's presence in your life. Reflect on the previous day, recognizing moments where you saw God at work, whether in challenges, joys, or mundane activities.

7. **Set Daily Intentions:** Based on your scripture reading and reflection, set one or two intentions for the day that align with your faith. This could involve showing kindness to a colleague, being patient with your family, or taking a step of faith in an area where you feel called.

8. **Offer Your Day to God:** Conclude your reflection time by offering your day and your intentions to God in prayer. Ask for His strength and guidance to live out your faith in all aspects of your day.

9. **Midday Check-In:** If possible, take a brief moment at midday to revisit your morning reflections and intentions. This can be a simple pause to remind yourself of your focus for the day and to sense God's presence.

10. **Evening Review:** At the end of the day, spend a few minutes reviewing your day in the context of your morning reflections and intentions. Acknowledge where you saw God at work and where you might have struggled to live out your faith. Offer a prayer of thanks for God's presence and ask for His grace for areas of challenge.

11. **Adjust as Needed:** Be flexible and open to adjusting your daily faith reflection routine as you discover what deepens your connection to God and integrates your faith more fully into daily life.

Exercise 2: Scripture-Based Goal Setting

Objective: To align personal goals with scripture, fostering a deeper connection with God's will and integrating faith into daily planning and aspirations.

Step-by-step instructions:

1. **Select a Quiet Time and Place:** Choose a calm and comfortable spot where you can focus without distractions. This setting should be conducive to reflection and prayer.

2. **Pray for Guidance:** Begin with a prayer, asking God to guide your thoughts and intentions as you set your goals. Seek clarity and alignment with His will for your life.

3. **Reflect on Your Values:** Consider the values that are most important to you in your faith journey. Write these down as they will form the foundation of your goal-setting process.

4. **Identify Key Areas for Growth:** Think about areas of your life where you wish to see growth or improvement that aligns with your faith values. Common areas might include spiritual growth, family relationships, career, health, or service to others.

5. **Choose Scripture for Each Area:** For each area of growth, select a scripture that resonates with your aspirations. For example, if focusing on patience, you might choose Galatians 5:22-23. Write the scripture next to each goal area.

6. **Set Specific Goals:** With your values, areas for growth, and scriptures in mind, set specific, measurable, achievable, relevant, and time-bound (SMART) goals. For instance, if your area of growth is spiritual, a goal might be to spend 15 minutes each morning in prayer and scripture reading.

7. **Create Action Steps:** Break down each goal into smaller action steps. If your goal is to read the Bible in a year, an action step could be to read for 20 minutes each day before bedtime.

8. **Incorporate into Daily Life:** Plan how to integrate these action steps into your daily routine. Use a planner, app, or journal to schedule your activities, ensuring that each goal is actively pursued.

9. **Review and Reflect Regularly:** Set aside time weekly or monthly to review your progress. Reflect on any challenges or successes, and consider how closely your actions align with the scripture and values you've chosen.

10. **Adjust as Needed:** Be open to adjusting your goals and action steps as you grow and as circumstances change. Remember, the aim is progress, not perfection, in aligning your life more closely with God's word.

11. **Share Your Journey:** Consider sharing your goals and the scriptures that guide them with a trusted friend or family member. This can provide accountability, encouragement, and shared spiritual growth.

12. **Offer Thanks:** Regularly thank God for His guidance and the progress you're making, even in small steps. Acknowledge His role in your achievements and seek His strength in areas where you're struggling.

Exercise 3: Faith-Driven Decision Making

Objective: To integrate faith into daily decision-making processes, empowering you to make choices that align with your spiritual values and God's guidance, thereby enhancing peace and balance in your life.

Step-by-step instructions:

1. **Identify the Decision:** Clearly define the decision you are facing. Write it down in a journal or piece of paper, specifying all aspects that are causing uncertainty or stress.

2. **Seek Scriptural Guidance:** Find scripture passages that relate to the nature of your decision. For example, if you're making a career decision, you might look at Proverbs 3:5-6. Write these passages down and meditate on their relevance to your situation.

3. **Pray for Wisdom:** Spend time in prayer, asking God to provide clarity and wisdom for the decision at hand. Be open to the Holy Spirit's guidance, seeking not just an answer but a peace about the direction you should take.

4. **List Pros and Cons:** Create a list of pros and cons for each option you're considering. Next to each item, note any scriptural insights or impressions from prayer that relate to these points, highlighting where your faith perspectives intersect with practical considerations.

5. **Consult Godly Counsel:** Seek advice from spiritually mature individuals who understand your faith values. Share your decision, scriptural insights, and what you've discerned through prayer, asking for their perspectives and any additional biblical principles that might apply.

6. **Imagine the Outcomes:** For each of your main options, spend time visualizing the potential outcomes, not just in practical terms but also how each choice aligns with your spiritual goals and God's kingdom. Consider how each decision might impact your ability to serve, grow in faith, and witness to others.

7. **Reflect on God's Peace:** After considering each option, reflect on which choice brings a sense of peace that aligns with Philippians 4:7. This peace, which transcends understanding, often indicates God's approval of a decision.

8. **Make a Tentative Choice:** Based on your analysis and spiritual discernment, make a tentative choice. Bring this decision before God in prayer, asking for confirmation or redirection according to His will.

9. **Look for Confirmation:** Be attentive to God's confirmation through His Word, circumstances, godly counsel, and the inner witness of the Holy Spirit in your heart. Confirmation may not always be dramatic; it can come through a growing sense of peace and assurance in your decision.

10. **Take Action with Faith:** Once you've received confirmation, take action with faith, trusting that God is guiding your steps. Document the process and outcome in your journal, noting any lessons learned or ways you saw God's hand at work.

11. **Offer Thanks and Praise:** Regardless of the outcome, give thanks to God for His guidance and presence throughout the decision-making process. Use this experience to grow in trust and reliance on Him, praising Him for His faithfulness in all circumstances.

Exercise 4: Morning Faith Ritual

Objective: To establish a morning ritual that centers your day around faith and spirituality, creating a foundation of peace and purpose from the moment you wake up. This practice aims to integrate your faith into the start of your day, ensuring that God's presence guides your thoughts, actions, and decisions from morning until night.

Step-by-step instructions:

1. **Select a Quiet Space:** Choose a quiet and comfortable spot in your home where you can be undisturbed for at least 15-20 minutes each morning. This could be a cozy chair by a window, a dedicated corner of your bedroom, or even your kitchen table before the rest of the household wakes up.

2. **Gather Inspirational Materials:** Prepare your space with items that inspire you and draw you into a mindset of worship and reflection. This may include your Bible, a devotional book, a journal, and a pen. Optionally, you can include a candle or soft instrumental music to enhance the atmosphere.

3. **Begin with Silence:** Start your ritual with a minute of silent meditation, focusing on your breathing to help clear your mind and center your thoughts on God's presence.

4. **Read Scripture:** Open your Bible and read a predetermined scripture passage. You might follow a Bible reading plan or select a verse that speaks to your current life circumstances. Allow the words to sink in, reading them multiple times if needed to fully grasp their significance.

5. **Reflect and Journal:** Spend a few minutes reflecting on the scripture you read. Journal your thoughts, feelings, and any insights you gain. Consider how the passage applies to your life and what actions or changes it inspires.

6. **Pray:** Engage in prayer, bringing your thoughts, concerns, and gratitude to God. Use this time to pray for your day ahead, your loved ones, and any specific needs or worries you have. Incorporate prayers of thanksgiving to cultivate a grateful heart.

7. **Set Daily Intentions:** Based on your scripture reading and prayer time, set one or two intentions for your day. These should be simple, achievable goals that align with your faith and the insights you've gained during your morning ritual.

8. **Close with Gratitude:** Conclude your morning faith ritual by expressing gratitude for God's unfailing love and the gift of a new day. Thank God for His guidance and ask for His presence to be with you throughout the day.

9. **Carry Your Faith Forward:** As you move into your day, keep a small reminder of your morning ritual with you—a verse written on a notecard, a meaningful token, or even a specific prayer in your heart. Let this reminder serve to bring you back to your intentions and God's presence throughout the day.

10. **Review and Adjust:** At the end of your day or week, take time to reflect on how your morning faith ritual has impacted your daily life and spirituality. Adjust your practice as needed to better meet your spiritual needs and deepen your relationship with God.

Exercise 5: Evening Gratitude Prayer

Objective: To foster a deeper connection with God and cultivate a heart of gratitude by reflecting on the day's blessings and challenges through an Evening Gratitude Prayer, reinforcing a spirit of thankfulness and reliance on God's guidance.

Step-by-step instructions:

1. **Set Aside a Quiet Time:** Choose a calm moment in the evening, ideally just before bedtime, to engage in this prayerful reflection. Ensure you are in a place where you can be undisturbed for a few minutes.

2. **Prepare Your Heart and Mind:** Begin by taking several deep breaths to center yourself. With each exhale, release any tension or stress from the day. Invite the Holy Spirit to guide this time of prayer and reflection.

3. **Acknowledge God's Presence:** Start your prayer by acknowledging God's constant presence in your life. Express gratitude for His love, protection, and provision throughout the day.

4. **Reflect on the Day's Blessings:** Think back on the day and identify three specific blessings or moments for which you are thankful. These can be as simple as a meaningful conversation, a moment of beauty in nature, or an instance where you felt God's guidance.

5. **Offer Thanks for Each Blessing:** For each blessing identified, offer a prayer of thanks to God. Detail why each moment was significant to you and how it demonstrated God's love and care.

6. **Contemplate the Day's Challenges:** Reflect on any challenges or difficulties you encountered during the day. Consider what lessons you can learn from these experiences and how they might be opportunities for growth or reliance on God.

7. **Seek Forgiveness and Healing:** If there were any moments of failure, sin, or missed opportunities to show love and kindness, confess these to God. Ask for His forgiveness and for the strength to do better.

8. **Pray for Others:** Bring before God the needs of others in your life—family, friends, colleagues, or anyone who is struggling. Ask God to meet their needs, provide comfort, and guide them according to His will.

9. **Ask for God's Guidance for Tomorrow:** Look ahead to the coming day. Ask for God's wisdom and guidance in any specific decisions or tasks you face. Pray for the strength to live according to His purposes and for opportunities to serve and bless others.

10. **Close in Praise:** Conclude your Evening Gratitude Prayer with words of praise for God's unchanging nature and His faithfulness. Reaffirm your trust in His good and perfect plans for your life.

11. **Journal Your Reflections (Optional):** After your prayer time, you may choose to journal about the insights or commitments that arose during your reflection. Writing down your prayers and God's faithfulness can be a powerful reminder of His work in your life.

Chapter 9: Embracing a Life of Serenity

As we continue to move forward in our quest for serenity, it is essential to focus on setting intentions that nurture a peaceful future. This involves a deliberate choice to prioritize practices that align with our faith and values, ensuring that every action we take contributes to our overall sense of peace and fulfillment. **Setting intentions** is not merely about goal-setting in the traditional sense; it is about aligning our deepest desires with God's plan for us, allowing His wisdom to guide our path.

Daily serenity planning routine becomes a crucial tool in this process. It involves starting each day with a moment of reflection, prayer, and meditation on God's word. This daily ritual helps to center our thoughts, focus our intentions, and surrender our plans to God's greater purpose. By doing so, we invite His peace to permeate our day, regardless of the challenges we may face.

Incorporating **serenity-enhancing time management** strategies is another vital step. This means prioritizing activities that feed our soul and bring us closer to God, while also managing our responsibilities and commitments in a way that reduces stress and anxiety. It could involve setting boundaries around work, dedicating specific times for prayer and family, or even saying no to commitments that detract from our spiritual well-being.

Exercise 1: Serenity-Focused Goal Setting encourages readers to reflect on their life's direction and how it aligns with their spiritual values. This exercise is about identifying areas where God's peace can be more deeply integrated into their lives, whether in relationships, work, or personal growth. It's about setting goals that are not just achievements but are reflections of a life lived in harmony with God's will.

Exercise 2: Daily Serenity Planning Routine guides readers through establishing a morning ritual that sets the tone for a serene day. This includes scripture reading, prayer, and meditation, focusing on God's promises of peace and guidance. By starting the day grounded in faith, readers can navigate the day's challenges with grace and peace.

Exercise 3: Serenity-Enhancing Time Management offers practical steps for integrating faith into the daily schedule. This involves identifying time-wasters and stressors and replacing them with activities that enhance spiritual well-being. It's about creating a balanced life where faith and daily responsibilities complement rather than conflict with each other.

These practices and exercises are designed to help readers not only pursue serenity but to live it out daily. By focusing on God's presence and promises, setting intentions that reflect His will, and managing our time in a way that honors Him, we can experience a profound sense of peace and fulfillment. This isn't just about overcoming anxiety or finding temporary calm; it's about embracing a life of serenity that flows from a deep, unshakeable trust in God.

Setting Intentions for Peace

Building on the foundation of setting intentions for a peaceful future, it becomes evident that these intentions must be deeply rooted in **faith** and the **daily application** of God's word. To live a life of serenity, one must not only set goals but also actively seek God's guidance in each step. This proactive approach involves **prayerful discernment** of God's will, **mindful engagement** with scripture, and the **intentional application** of biblical principles in daily life.

Prayerful discernment is a critical aspect of setting intentions that align with God's plan. It involves seeking God's guidance through prayer, especially when making decisions or facing challenges. This process allows individuals to surrender their plans and desires to God, trusting in His wisdom and timing. By doing so, they can navigate life with a sense of peace, knowing that they are following a path that is divinely ordained.

Mindful engagement with scripture is another essential practice. It involves not just reading the Bible but meditating on its verses, allowing God's word to sink deep into the heart and mind. This engagement fosters a deeper understanding of God's character and promises, which in turn shapes one's perspective and reactions to life's situations. It is through this deep connection with scripture that individuals can find strength, guidance, and comfort in times of anxiety and uncertainty.

Intentional application of biblical principles in daily life is the natural progression of setting intentions grounded in faith. It means putting into practice the teachings and values found in scripture, such as love, forgiveness, patience, and gratitude. This application is not limited to personal growth but extends to interactions with others, influencing relationships, work, and community involvement. By living out these principles, individuals can become beacons of God's peace and love in a troubled world.

Exercise 1: Serenity-Focused Goal Setting not only invites readers to contemplate their life's direction but also challenges them to identify specific, actionable steps to integrate God's peace into every aspect of their lives. This might include setting aside daily time for scripture reading and prayer, committing to acts of service, or cultivating relationships that encourage spiritual growth.

Exercise 2: Daily Serenity Planning Routine emphasizes the importance of beginning each day with a focus on God's presence and promises. This routine can help set the tone for the day, ensuring that every decision and interaction is infused with a sense of calm and purpose. It also serves as a reminder that, no matter what the day brings, God's peace is always accessible.

Exercise 3: Serenity-Enhancing Time Management offers practical advice for balancing spiritual priorities with daily responsibilities. This involves identifying priorities that align with one's faith and values, setting boundaries to protect time for spiritual practices, and being mindful of how one's activities contribute to or detract from a sense of peace.

Through these practices and exercises, readers are equipped to not only set intentions for a peaceful future but to actively cultivate a life characterized by serenity and faithfulness. By prioritizing a relationship with God and applying His word in every area of life, individuals can experience the profound peace and joy that comes from living in alignment with His will. This approach to setting intentions ensures that every aspect of life is infused with purpose, hope, and tranquility, reflecting the deep peace that transcends understanding.

Continuing with Confidence and Faith

Prayerful discernment is not merely a task but a lifestyle. It calls for a daily commitment to seeking the Lord's guidance, particularly in moments of decision-making or when facing uncertainties. This discernment is cultivated through persistent prayer, a practice that not only draws one closer to God but also sharpens the ability to hear His voice. By integrating prayerful discernment into daily routines, individuals can navigate life's challenges with a sense of divine direction and assurance.

Mindful engagement with scripture goes beyond casual reading. It involves an intentional dive into the Word, allowing it to penetrate the heart and transform the mind. This engagement is a form of meditation where one not only reads but also reflects on the scriptures, seeking to understand God's character and His promises. Such a practice can significantly impact one's perspective, offering comfort and guidance in times of anxiety and equipping individuals with wisdom for life's journey.

Intentional application of biblical principles in daily life is the natural outcome of a heart transformed by the Word. This application is about living out the teachings of scripture in every aspect of life, from personal interactions to professional endeavors. It involves practicing love, forgiveness, patience, and gratitude, thereby embodying the principles of the Kingdom of God. Through this application, individuals can influence their surroundings positively, promoting peace and harmony in their communities.

Exercise 1: Serenity-Focused Goal Setting challenges individuals to align their life goals with their faith, encouraging them to consider how each goal reflects their relationship with God and contributes to their spiritual growth. This exercise prompts deep reflection on personal aspirations, guiding individuals to set goals that not only bring personal fulfillment but also glorify God.

Exercise 2: Daily Serenity Planning Routine emphasizes the importance of beginning each day with a focus on God. This routine is about setting aside time each morning for prayer, scripture reading, and meditation, creating a foundation of peace and purpose for the day ahead. By starting the day in God's presence, individuals can approach their daily tasks with calmness and clarity, rooted in the assurance of His guidance.

Exercise 3: Serenity-Enhancing Time Management offers practical strategies for integrating one's faith into the hustle and bustle of daily life. This exercise encourages individuals to evaluate their daily activities, identifying those that contribute to their spiritual well-being and those that do not. By prioritizing activities that foster a closer relationship with God and setting boundaries to protect time for spiritual practices, individuals can maintain a sense of peace amidst their responsibilities.

Through these exercises and practices, readers are equipped to continue their journey with confidence and faith. By prioritizing their relationship with God and applying His Word in every area of their lives, they can navigate the complexities of life with a profound sense of peace and purpose. This approach ensures that every decision, interaction, and challenge is met with a heart grounded in faith and a mind focused on God's promises, leading to a life characterized by serenity and fulfillment.

3 Exercises for Everyday Serenity

Exercise 1: Serenity-Focused Goal Setting

Objective: To align personal and spiritual goals with a focus on serenity, utilizing scripture and prayer to guide the goal-setting process for a peaceful and purposeful life.

Step-by-step instructions:

1. **Identify Areas of Life Needing Serenity:** Reflect on aspects of your life where stress and anxiety are most prevalent. Consider categories such as work, family, health, spirituality, and personal growth.

2. **Select Scriptures That Speak to Serenity:** Choose scriptures that resonate with your desire for peace and calm in the identified areas. For instance, Philippians 4:6-7 can be comforting for anxiety-related goals.

3. **Pray for Guidance:** Before setting any goals, spend a moment in prayer, asking for God's guidance to align your aspirations with His will and for the wisdom to pursue goals that lead to true serenity.

4. **Set Specific, Measurable Goals:** For each area identified, set specific and measurable goals. For example, if seeking serenity in work, a goal might be to dedicate 10 minutes of every workday to silent prayer or scripture reading to center yourself.

5. **Incorporate Scripture into Your Goals:** Attach a piece of scripture to each goal as a spiritual anchor. Write down how each scripture passage supports your goal and how it will remind you of God's promises of peace.

6. **Develop Action Steps:** Break down each goal into actionable steps. If your goal is to reduce stress through better health, one step could be to walk for 30 minutes three times a week while meditating on your chosen scripture.

7. **Create a Serenity Journal:** Start a journal dedicated to tracking your progress. Include your goals, the scripture you've chosen, and daily or weekly reflections on your journey towards serenity.

8. **Schedule Regular Reviews:** Set a weekly or monthly time to review your goals and progress. Use this time to reflect on the peace you've experienced, adjustments needed for your goals, and to offer prayers of thanksgiving for God's guidance.

9. **Seek Accountability:** Share your goals with a trusted friend or family member who can offer support, encouragement, and accountability. Discuss the scriptures you've chosen and how they're guiding your path to serenity.

10. **Practice Gratitude:** At the end of each day, write down at least one thing you're grateful for in your serenity journal. Focusing on gratitude can shift your perspective from anxiety to peace.

11. **Adjust Goals as Needed:** Be flexible and open to the Holy Spirit's leading. If you find certain goals aren't bringing the peace you sought, pray for direction and adjust your goals accordingly.

Exercise 2: Daily Serenity Planning Routine

Objective: To establish a routine that prioritizes serenity and peace through deliberate planning, integrating faith into daily activities and reflections to create a balanced, serene life.

Step-by-step instructions:

1. **Begin with Prayer:** Start your planning session by praying for guidance. Ask God to help you prioritize your day according to His will, seeking peace and balance in every task and commitment.

2. **Reflect on Scripture:** Choose a scripture that speaks to peace and serenity, such as Philippians 4:6-7. Meditate on this verse, allowing it to set a peaceful tone for your planning.

3. **Review Your Calendar:** Look at your schedule for the day ahead. Identify essential tasks and appointments, as well as any time slots that lack a specific purpose.

4. **Set Serenity Goals:** For each main part of your day (morning, afternoon, evening), set a goal that promotes serenity. This could be as simple as dedicating 15 minutes to silence, reading a devotional, or taking a walk to connect with nature.

5. **Incorporate Acts of Faith:** Plan at least one activity that strengthens your faith, such as attending a Bible study, volunteering, or writing in a gratitude journal. Position this activity at a time when you typically feel most stressed or disconnected.

6. **Allocate Time for Reflection:** Schedule a brief period for reflection at the end of the day. Use this time to review how well you integrated serenity and faith into your routine and to note any adjustments for the following day.

7. **Plan for Flexibility:** Recognize that unexpected tasks or challenges may arise. Decide in advance to approach these with a calm and prayerful mindset, asking for God's peace in every situation.

8. **Prepare for Tomorrow:** Conclude your planning session by preparing anything you might need for tomorrow's serenity goals. This could involve gathering reading materials, setting out walking shoes, or writing a prayer intention for the day.

9. **Close with Thankfulness:** End your planning routine with a prayer of thanksgiving, acknowledging God's presence in your planning process and entrusting your plans to Him.

10. **Review Weekly:** At the end of each week, take time to review your daily serenity planning routines. Assess what worked well, what brought the most peace, and what could be improved. Adjust your planning process accordingly to better meet your serenity goals.

Exercise 3: Serenity-Enhancing Time Management

Objective: Enhance daily serenity and manage time effectively by integrating faith into your planning routine, ensuring that your daily activities align with your spiritual values and contribute to a peaceful life balance.

Step-by-step instructions:

1. **Begin with Prayer:** Start your planning session by praying for guidance. Ask God to help you prioritize your tasks according to His will and to grant you wisdom in managing your time effectively.

2. **List Your Daily Tasks:** Write down all the tasks you need or want to accomplish in a day. Include everything from work obligations and household chores to personal goals and time for rest.

3. **Categorize Your Tasks:** Group your tasks into categories such as 'Essential', 'Important but not Urgent', and 'Optional'. This will help you see where your priorities lie and how you might need to adjust them.

4. **Assign Time Blocks:** Allocate specific time blocks for each task or category of tasks. Be realistic about how much time each task will take, and remember to include breaks and moments for reflection.

5. **Incorporate Faith Activities:** Make sure to include time for prayer, scripture reading, or other faith-based activities. These are essential for maintaining serenity and should be treated as non-negotiable parts of your day.

6. **Set Boundaries:** Decide on a time in the evening when you will cease all work-related activities. This boundary will help ensure you have time to unwind and focus on family, faith, and rest.

7. **Review and Adjust:** At the end of your planning, review your schedule. Ask yourself if it reflects a balance between work, personal growth, faith, and rest. Make adjustments as necessary to ensure it aligns with your spiritual values and serenity goals.

8. **Seek God's Affirmation:** Once your plan feels balanced, pray over your schedule. Ask for God's affirmation or any nudges to adjust your plans further. Be open to the Holy Spirit's guidance, which may prompt you to make changes.

9. **Implement with Flexibility:** Approach your day with the planned schedule but remain flexible. Unexpected tasks or opportunities to serve others may arise, and these can also be important moments where God is leading you.

10. **Reflect at Day's End:** Spend a few minutes in the evening reflecting on how your day went. Consider what tasks brought you peace and which ones may have detracted from it. Use this reflection to inform your planning for the next day.

11. **Express Gratitude:** End your day by thanking God for His guidance and the strength provided to accomplish your tasks. Acknowledge any moments where you felt His presence particularly strongly, and express gratitude for the peace experienced throughout the day.

Conclusion

In the pursuit of serenity, one of the most transformative realizations is that peace does not come from external circumstances but from a deep, unwavering faith in God's providence. This understanding is crucial for those who find themselves caught in the whirlwind of daily life, juggling responsibilities, and facing challenges that seem insurmountable. The key to unlocking this lasting peace lies in the intentional practice of turning every worry, every ambition, and every dream over to God, trusting that His plans are to prosper and not to harm. **Trust in God** becomes not just a concept but a daily lived experience, a foundation upon which a life of serenity is built.

Daily reflection on God's word is an essential practice for nurturing this trust. By immersing oneself in scripture, individuals are reminded of God's unchanging nature, His infinite wisdom, and His boundless love for His children. This daily habit serves as a spiritual anchor, keeping one grounded in the midst of life's storms. It's a practice that transforms not only the individual's heart and mind but also their approach to life's challenges, enabling them to face each day with confidence and grace.

Gratitude plays a pivotal role in this journey toward serenity. Recognizing and appreciating God's gifts, even in the midst of trials, shifts the focus from what is lacking to the abundance that exists. This shift in perspective is powerful, fostering a sense of contentment and joy that transcends circumstances. By cultivating a heart of gratitude, individuals can experience the peace of God that surpasses all understanding, a peace that guards hearts and minds in Christ Jesus.

Community support is another critical component of finding serenity. Sharing the journey with others who are also seeking to deepen their faith and live out God's promises provides encouragement, accountability, and a sense of belonging. Whether through small group studies, prayer meetings, or simply doing life together, these relationships are a source of strength and comfort. They remind individuals that they are not alone, that they are part of a larger body of believers who are walking the same path toward peace and fulfillment in God.

As we delve deeper into the practices that foster serenity, it's important to remember that this is not a journey of perfection but of progress. Each step taken in faith, each moment spent in prayer, each scripture verse meditated upon brings us closer to the peace God promises. It's a process of learning to lean not on our own understanding but on God's, of surrendering our will to His, and of finding rest in His sovereignty. This process is ongoing, a lifelong journey of growing closer to God and discovering the depths of the peace He offers.

Prayerful surrender emerges as a vital practice in cultivating a serene life. This act of yielding one's desires, fears, and plans to God in prayer is both liberating and empowering. It acknowledges God's supreme authority and wisdom, entrusting every aspect of our lives to His care. Through prayerful surrender, individuals open themselves to receive God's guidance, comfort, and peace, which in turn, helps navigate life's uncertainties with a steadfast heart. This practice underscores the belief that God is in control and that His plans are always for our good, even when circumstances suggest otherwise.

Mindfulness and presence in the moment are crucial for recognizing God's hand in our daily lives. In the rush to accomplish tasks and meet deadlines, it's easy to overlook the quiet ways in which God speaks to us and leads us. By slowing down and being fully present, we become more attuned to the subtle yet profound ways God is at work. Whether it's through the beauty of nature, the kindness of a stranger, or the unexpected resolution of a problem, acknowledging God's presence in these moments strengthens our faith and deepens our sense of peace.

Service and giving reflect the heart of God and play a significant role in experiencing serenity. By focusing on the needs of others and extending ourselves in service, we shift our perspective from our own worries and challenges to the broader picture of God's kingdom work. This act of selflessness mirrors Jesus' life on earth and draws us closer to Him. It also provides a profound sense of purpose and fulfillment, knowing that we are making a tangible difference in the lives of others through God's love.

Spiritual accountability with a trusted friend or mentor is invaluable in maintaining a path toward serenity. This relationship offers support, encouragement, and gentle correction when necessary, helping keep our focus on God and His promises. It serves as a reminder of our commitment to live according to God's word and to persevere in faith, even when faced with obstacles. Spiritual accountability ensures that we are not journeying alone but are supported by others who share our desire for a deeper relationship with God.

In embracing these practices, it's essential to approach them with patience and grace, giving ourselves permission to grow at our own pace. The path to serenity is unique for each individual, filled with its own set of challenges and victories. However, the underlying principle remains the same: a life anchored in faith, lived in accordance with God's word, and surrendered to His will, is a life where true serenity can be found. As we commit to these practices, we can trust that God will meet us where we are, guiding us gently toward the peace that only He can provide.

www.ingramcontent.com/pod-product-compliance
Lightning Source LLC
Chambersburg PA
CBHW062048090426
42740CB00016B/3063